Outdoor Living with Style

Home MAGAZINE
Outdoor Living with Style

Foreword by Gale C. Steves,
Editor-in-Chief of HOME® Magazine

Ellen M. Plante

FRIEDMAN/FAIRFAX
PUBLISHERS

A FRIEDMAN/FAIRFAX BOOK

Please visit our website: www.metrobooks.com

© 2001, 1999 by Michael Friedman Publishing Group, Inc.

HOME® is a registered trademark of Hachette Filipacchi Magazines II, Inc.

Library of Congress Cataloging-in-Publication Data available upon request.

ISBN 1-58663-159-4

Special Thanks to Timothy Drew
Editor: Reka Simonsen
Art Director: Jeff Batzli
Designer: Andrea Karman
Photography Editor: Wendy Missan
Production Manager: Camille Lee

Color separations by Bright Arts Graphics (S) Pte Ltd
Printed in China by Leefung-Asco Printers Ltd.

1 3 5 7 9 10 8 6 4 2

Distributed by Sterling Publishing Company, Inc.
387 Park Avenue South
New York, NY 10016
Distributed in Canada by Sterling Publishing
Canadian Manda Group
One Atlantic Avenue, Suite 105
Toronto, Ontario, Canada M6K 3E7
Distributed in Australia by
Capricorn Link (Australia) Pty Ltd.
P.O. Box 6651
Baulkham Hills, Business Centre, NSW 2153, Australia

Contents

If we were to ask one hundred HOME® readers to describe their ideal outdoor living spaces, I'm sure we would get one hundred very different answers. For one, it might be the quintessential patio fitted out with the latest barbecue equipment and ready to accommodate the annual family reunion. For another, it's a vine-covered pergola set in a well-tended garden where a chaise longue and a wrought-iron table make an ideal spot for reading a good book—or dozing—with a glass of lemonade at the ready.

Yet, despite our individual interpretations of what an outdoor living space should be, there is a common thread in all of these descriptions. What we are all looking for in our homes is a way to create an outdoor area that in many ways functions as an indoor space where we can relax, play, entertain, or simply take pleasure in being able to smell the roses. A lesson that HOME's readers have learned is that one way to extend the square footage of our homes is to bring indoor

comforts and amenities out into the open air. Build an airy gazebo in the garden and you have the perfect spot to watch the butterflies give way to fireflies in the last light of day. It's not the backyard, per se; it's the amenities you add and how you "furnish" it that transform it into a warm-weather living or dining room.

Of course, it's impossible to generalize about such a broad topic when so much depends on personal tastes and goals, not to mention the variety of climates across the continent. Residents of the Sun Belt are blessed with a climate that affords them the opportunity to fully blend indoor and outdoor living. While our readers in the more northerly latitudes may not have endless summer, perhaps the brevity of the season makes their appreciation all the more intense. And besides, when it comes to bridging the seasonal gap, they've learned a trick or two. Sunrooms and greenhouse rooms, for example, aren't truly out of doors, but they can be made to feel as if they are.

Apart from letting your imagination take flight, there are some practical considerations to keep in mind. Whether your vision is a rustic bower set in an old-fashioned garden or a sleek poolside patio, you'll need to give some thought to how you want to furnish and decorate it, how it should be lit, what you need to do to make it safe, and what measures to take for maximum privacy. Whatever your goals, we have designed HOME Magazine's *Outdoor Living with Style* to help you see the possibilities and master the details, so that when you're done, you'll have created the space that suits you and your family perfectly.

Gale C. Steves
Editor-in-Chief, HOME® Magazine

Stained a warm honey color, this beautiful deck coordinates perfectly with rattan furnishings. A ledge has been fashioned to separate the deck from the surrounding embankment and serves as handy seating or a display spot for statuary, figurines, or even potted plants. Plump cushions add comfort to the chairs, and select objets d'art are arranged on the tabletop. Nature takes center stage here, so little else is called for to enhance the decorative effect.

Realizing the full potential of our homes is often a challenge and certainly an ongoing endeavor. Our needs are subject to change; we start a family and then before we know it, children are grown and gone, work is increasingly being done at home, and today's high-tech entertainment and exercise equipment demand space of their own. The one constant in our home life is the need and desire for outdoor living areas that provide space for relaxation, quiet contemplation, recreation, and entertaining. Making the most of outdoor spaces—which can be year-round or seasonal extensions of the home—is what this book is all about. Regardless of whether you're building from scratch or remodeling an existing porch or backyard deck, transitional spaces between indoors and out can provide the means to live large, even in the most modest space. And rest assured that space constraints needn't prove a roadblock. The high-rise apartment balcony or freestanding garden

Introduction

gazebo can be every bit as lovely, functional, and enjoyable as an old-fashioned veranda or spacious brick patio. All it takes is careful planning to meet your needs and an eye toward comfortable, inviting, and attractive design.

The pages that follow explore the stylish outdoor living spaces we love best: front porches, screened porches, backyard decks, poolside patios, balconies and rooftop terraces, inviting garden retreats, and conservatories, as well as sunrooms or greenhouse rooms. Your individual needs, the family budget, available space, and your home's architectural design will all influence your choice. Any of these outdoor "rooms" will not only expand your existing living space but will add to the beauty of your home and the value of your property. Many of the practical aspects associated with designing and building a handsome outdoor living space are included here, but the primary concern is to find ways to turn any outdoor space into a *living* space—one that will be convenient and a joy to use. With this in mind, read on to discover ideas for furnishing outdoor spaces, adding decorative elements, creating privacy and garden accents, entertaining alfresco, and landscaping to frame or enhance an outdoor space, as well as recreational options. Welcome to HOME Magazine's *Outdoor Living with Style*. May it help you create your own ideal outdoor sanctuary.

An alcove shielded from the elements offers an arched view of the surrounding
countryside. A long wooden table, positioned for full enjoyment of the scenery,
is casually set with glasses for cool drinks. You can almost hear
the birds singing and feel the soft breeze.

As the quintessential American outdoor living space, the front porch has been an important architectural element in vernacular home design for well over two hundred years. The classic front porch reached the height of popularity during the late 1800s—the  Victorian age—when this transitional space between the prim and proper indoors and the beauty of the outside world was considered an ideal and informal place to entertain. Perhaps more important, this outdoor parlor of sorts was also the perfect spot to reap the healthful benefits of fresh air and just the right amount of sunshine.

A traditional feature of homes in the American South, a double-height porch makes a beautiful architectural statement and provides abundant space for enjoying the outdoors, as well as fresh breezes on warm days when windows and doors are thrown open to the air.

A descendant of the ancient portico (a roof-covered colonnade), the front porch began to appear across the North American landscape in large numbers between 1840 and 1930. Numerous architectural pattern books made affordable home designs readily available and increased the popularity of certain architectural styles, such as the Queen Anne of the late 1800s with its abundance of ornamental gingerbread on porches and façades. Thanks to these pattern books and to home "kits" that could be mail-ordered and then delivered via the railway to depots near building sites, front porches were literally everywhere. Even the middle-class bungalow-style home of the early twentieth century, that architectural gem born of the Arts and Crafts movement, routinely incorporated the all-important front porch into its architectural design. After that, however, the 1930s and 1940s saw the popularity of several revival styles in home building (sans front porch) and the move to the suburbs, which made the front porch obsolete and terribly old-fashioned.

Fortunately, the front porch is back today and more beautiful than ever. Due in part to the historical preservation movement in communities everywhere, we've realized the significant value of nineteenth-century architecture and the role that these historic homes—with their handsome front porches—played in the community at large. In addition, modern-day efforts to reclaim community spirit have seen the rise of numerous "planned communities" where homes are designed with front porches to encourage neighborliness. And yet another point worth noting is that as homes are increasingly viewed as our refuges from a bustling, high-tech world, we want those homes to be as comfortable and pleasing as possible. It's no secret that a well-designed front porch can turn a nondescript house into an eye-catching home, increase property value, and extend living space all at the same time.

OPPOSITE: Twin rustic rockers are perfect for relaxing and enjoying the late afternoon sun. A small table keeps cool drinks handy while a ceiling fan, always a plus on the porch, helps keep the fresh air circulating. Wirework plant stands are a wonderful decorative touch in an outdoor living space thanks to their delicate design.

ABOVE: A spacious veranda wraps around this lovely Queen Anne home, serving as both a front and a side porch. The delicate fretwork near the ceiling is a beautiful example of the gingerbread trim that the Victorians were so fond of. Graceful balusters and porch supports contribute a light, airy feeling.

Creating the Perfect Front Porch

The front porch can be a multifunctional, stylish living space regardless of whether you are building from scratch or remodeling an existing porch, but in both cases there are some practical considerations you'll want to keep in mind. First and foremost, spend some time thinking about your lifestyle to determine exactly what purpose your porch will serve. Do you envision the porch as a safe play area for small children? Will it be used for casual entertaining? Do you see it primarily as a restful spot for family and neighbors to gather? Beyond the attractive "face-lift" it can give your home, the porch can be utilized in many ways. Make a list of possible uses and utilize that list to help plan a porch that will meet your every need.

Here, a modern architectural design makes full use of space to create a set back porch. Filled with wooden furnishings painted a cheery yellow, this porch provides plenty of room for a relaxing meal or a few moments stolen in a rocking chair. Red geraniums in terra-cotta pots enhance the festive, welcoming air.

Next, consider the architectural style of your home. Vintage buildings call for a porch that's histori-cally accurate and blends effortlessly with the rest of the home. For example, in renovating the portico or porch on a Greek Revival–style farmhouse, the columns (Ionic or Doric) used to support the porch roof become the focal point, while restoration of a porch on a lovely Victorian Stick–style house would make full use of porch posts sporting decorative diagonal braces and railings composed of intricate stick patterns. Research the history of an older home by contacting the local historical society and scouring books on period architecture to help you determine what's appropriate in the way of a front porch.

This handsome porch offers such a majestic view that little is needed to enhance the surroundings. Rugged porch flooring is joined by a wood-finished ceiling, white porch trim, and a wooden railing with iron balusters. A few well-chosen accessories, such as a primitive bench and several baskets of flowers, reinforce the rustic theme.

For homeowners considering the addition of a porch to a suburban ranch house, a split-level, a cozy Cape Cod, or a contemporary build, calling upon an architect or design service is a smart idea. After all, you're not just gaining outdoor living space by adding on a porch, you're also altering the shape and appearance of your home. Meet with several architects if need be until you find one who accurately envisions your concept of this all-important space. It's important to have a budget in mind for such a project and it's always wise to contact your local building inspector to inquire about property setbacks, restrictions, and the need for building permits.

When discussing the front porch there are actually three different types to consider. The open front porch graces the front of the home and may or may not have a series of columns or posts, a railing, and a stairway. A wraparound porch, or veranda, differs from the typical front porch in that it's generally wider and featured along the front and one side of the house in an L shape. A veranda has the advantage of increased space, two different views (perhaps one public and the other a bit more private), and increased cooling for the home's interior. Wraparound porches or verandas are especially popular in warm climates where outdoor living space can be enjoyed year-round. A third style, referred to as a setback porch, is often incorporated at the back of a home but can be an innovative way of using space and dressing the façade when used in conjunction with the front entryway.

ABOVE: Sometimes less is more on the porch when the ocean or a secluded lake is just beyond the front door. This spacious porch incorporates both covered and open areas, and furnishings can be moved as needed. What better spot to enjoy an alfresco meal?

OPPOSITE: A modern interpretation of the wraparound porch or veranda, this idyllic setting offers covered areas with two different views. The home's cedar-shake siding is accented with dark green trim and Adirondack chairs painted to match. Large clay pots are filled with small pine trees, geraniums, and annual vines.

Since the vast majority of porches are constructed from wood, when building, renovating, or simply maintaining, keep in mind that pressure-treated lumber will help assure longevity. Air flow beneath the porch and stairs is important to guard against moisture problems that cause wood to deteriorate. The porch floor should be built with a slight pitch so that water won't pool. The manner in which the wood is finished is also an important consideration. You can opt for a wood stain, a clear preservative, or paint. Oil- and water-based paints and enamel paints are available in high- or low-gloss finishes and a wide variety of colors. If you are doing the work yourself, it's worth spending time at the local home-building center to determine the proper finish for a porch in your region. If, on the other hand, you've hired a contractor to build or restore your porch, discuss these options with him or her.

While wood is often the main ingredient in porch construction, there are some alternatives to be considered. Columns today are also made of aluminum, and latticework, which is popular for porch skirting, is available in wood or durable PVC (polyvinyl chloride). Terra-cotta tiles, ceramic tiles, and stone (slate or granite) are other popular options when it comes to

A grouping of white Adirondack chairs blends effortlessly with white porch walls and trim and gray painted flooring to create the ideal outdoor room. Potted ferns, baskets filled with colorful blooms, and plump chair pillows encourage lingering with family and friends or just relaxing with a good book.

porch flooring. Given the wide range of colors and designs available, any of the above can be a practical and beautiful alternative to wood. Just be sure to select tile or stone that has a textured finish to prevent the floor from becoming slippery when wet.

These decisions, along with those you make regarding appropriate design elements for your porch (such as spindles for the railing, columns or posts, capitals and bases for columns, bric-a-brac, or decorative trim), will determine the finished look of your outdoor living space.

Once your front porch has been built or given that much-needed face-lift, it's time to really start thinking of it as a room. You'd give plenty of thought to furnishing and decorating the living room or family room, and the porch deserves the same consideration. Think of the flooring, ceiling, railings, and other design elements as the backdrop, and select colors that will set the stage for the porch you envision. Typically the porch is painted to match the trim color on the house (often white), but a wood finish may be more appropriate to a rustic dwelling; pastels and earth tones can be used as accent colors on Victorian Revival homes; and for a contemporary building, bolder colors are often preferred. Wooden porch flooring is often gray or some medium hue for practical purposes, and porch ceilings can run the gamut from white or sky blue to almost any pale tint. Tongue-and-groove or beadboard ceilings are often treated with a wood stain or preservative finish.

This Mexican hideaway comes complete with a tiled porch that offers cool relief from the heat and unforgettable views of the landscape. Handsome wooden furnishings wear a soft patina acquired over time, and accessories such as metalwork light fixtures, artwork, and potted ferns contribute elegant, old-world style.

Porch Swings and Rocking Chairs

Today there is a variety of outdoor furnishings to select from when outfitting the front porch. New weather-resistant materials and finishes combined with an abundance of styles make choices almost limitless. Do you adore the old-fashioned, romantic look of wicker or are you drawn to rugged and

ABOVE: An inviting porch swing and a pitcher of fresh lemonade—what more could you ask for? Porch swings have been a favorite furnishing for years, proving that a good idea never goes out of fashion. This particular swing is all the more endearing because of its timeworn finish, and the paint-chipped stool serving as a miniature table just happens to be the perfect accent.

OPPOSITE: This spacious porch is the ideal spot for entertaining friends. A trellis-style roof allows sunlight to filter through and is ideal in a warm climate. Wicker furnishings with comfy cushions are lovely in outdoor areas, provided the pieces are of the weather-resistant variety. As always, containers full of flowers reinforce an outdoor decorating scheme.

handsome woods? Options abound; there are also high-tech plastics (called resins) that look like wood and metals such as aluminum that can be given any number of colorful finishes.

Regarding wood furnishings appropriate for outdoor use, teak is by far the most durable—and the most costly. As it ages, teak will develop a beautiful silver-gray patina that gives furniture an elegant, timeless appeal. Redwood and pressure-treated pine are also popular for outdoor furniture construction, and they too can be allowed to "weather" naturally or can be treated with a protective sealer or painted finish. To help assure many enjoyable years of porch pleasure, wood furnishings should be stored away in the basement, garage, or shed during the winter months in colder climates.

When it comes to wicker—a catch-all word used to describe rattan, bamboo, reed, and machine-made paper-fiber furniture—save grandmother's heirloom pieces for indoor use and invest in modern, weatherized chairs, settees, tables, and so on for the open-air front porch. Several notable furniture manufacturers specialize in wicker that's been treated specifically for outdoor use, and they offer colorful, fade-resistant acrylic-covered cushions for added comfort.

This is the quintessential front porch, complete with Victorian gingerbread trim, hanging ferns, and vintage rockers waiting to provide serious rest and relaxation. This homey setting is proof positive that simplicity can indeed be lovely.

Afternoon Tea on the Front Porch

* Plan an English-style afternoon tea, complete with assorted delicate finger sandwiches. Cucumber with butter and smoked salmon with cream cheese are traditional favorites.

* Serve freshly brewed tea and homemade lemonade along with a selection of desserts such as trifle, scones with cream and jam, miniature tarts, and fresh fruit.

* Accessorize the porch table with a damask or lace tablecloth or a floral-patterned cloth and napkins.

* Have on hand a medley of colored glass luncheon plates or dessert plates, tumblers, and teacups. For a garden theme, use mixed or matched floral china dishes or pottery in muted shades.

* Make sure to have bouquets of fresh roses or sweet peas on the table.

This modern wicker furniture is produced in styles reminiscent of the Victorian age and the Arts and Crafts movement, as well as in contemporary designs.

While we usually think of metal furnishings as being more appropriate for the backyard deck or patio, there are so many designs available today that metal furnishings are finding their way onto the porch. Beautiful wrought- and cast-aluminum tables, chairs, benches, and chaise longues are produced in styles ranging from Victorian whimsy and European ambience to classical and modern renditions. They offer the advantage of numerous colored finishes and a wide selection of cushion designs.

And what about plastic furniture? Forget those preconceived notions of ugly, flimsy, cheap items. Today's high-tech plastic—polyethylene—will stand up to weather, sunlight, and chemicals and can be molded into a variety of shapes and styles. As a less costly alternative to wood, wicker, and metal furnishings, plastic can be the ideal way to outfit a porch attractively on a modest budget.

Once you've decided on the material for your porch furnishings, consider style—traditional, contemporary, rustic, Victorian, country, and so on. You'll also need to give thought to the individual furniture pieces you select. Since the porch usually serves several different purposes, a variety of comfortable chairs and a few small tables are called for. And when it comes to seating, the rocker—that venerable porch favorite—is always a welcome addition. Other options, if room allows, include a table for casual meals or refreshments, perhaps a chaise longue for enjoying a good book on a lazy afternoon, and even a porch swing for simply taking in the view. Other possibilities, especially if the porch will be occupied by children, include pint-size wooden or wicker chairs and a wicker trunk that can do double-duty as a coffee table and a toy box.

For solid comfort, outfit porch seating with plump, weather-resistant cushions. As a design element, the colors and patterns of the fabric you select can enhance the mood of your front porch. Do you want your porch to appear bright and cheerful, romantic, handsomely rugged, or thoroughly modern? Soft florals will help give the porch an outdoors theme that recalls the English countryside or a hint of the Victorian age. Bright stripes, on the other hand, have a playful, casual air. Most cushion fabrics for outdoor use are either polyester that's been treated with a vinyl coating or acrylic. Both are weather-resistant and a good choice for the front porch. Save delicate fabrics for the screened porch or sunroom where weather won't be an important factor. As an added decorative touch, a few throw pillows on the porch swing, rocker, or settee will make seating all the more inviting.

A generous porch accommodates a medley of furnishings for relaxing, entertaining, and dining. A pair of teak chaise longues are dressed with comfy cushions, while tables at either end are set for an outdoor meal. A cushioned settee and a wooden trunk used as a coffee table create an ideal spot for conversation—which can go long into the night, thanks to the candles and outdoor lighting fixtures.

Porch Lights and Details

Without a doubt your furnishings will claim center stage on the front porch, but there are other decorative elements that will heighten the visual appeal and homey comfort of this outdoor living space. For example, when it comes to lighting, select wall-mounted fixtures to flank both sides of the front door. These can be chosen based on the architectural style of your home or according to personal taste and should provide soft—not glaring—lighting. Fixtures can be as simple or elaborate as you like and are available in a wide array of designs and finishes. A historic home may call for attractive onion lanterns with a black or antiqued brass finish or perhaps verdigris signal lanterns, while a contemporary home is well suited to an inverted wall-mounted fixture with a beveled glass globe. This form of accent lighting not only illuminates the entryway but provides localized porch lighting.

General lighting, too, is an important consideration on the front porch and is usually achieved with ceiling lights. Again, choices are almost limitless and popular options include ceiling fixtures, recessed lighting, and pendant or drop fixtures. Regardless of what you choose, make sure your fixture blends with the ceiling and doesn't create a glaring contrast. Also, in many areas of the country a ceiling fan is a necessity on the front porch, and many models include lighting fixtures.

To control the intensity of light—sunlight, that is—you may decide to invest in colorful fabric awnings for the front porch. This can be quite beneficial if your porch has a southern exposure and receives a great deal of sun during the day. Fabric awnings are not only practical, they can also be very decorative and add a splash of bright color or fun-loving stripes to your home's façade. Fabric awnings are generally custom-made and available in stationary or retractable models. Durable and waterproof, they come in several different fabric types in varying price ranges to fit your budget.

Another popular porch accessory for filtering sunlight is bamboo or matchstick blinds, or plastic counterparts that look like bamboo. The do-it-yourselfer can easily take measurements and then shop at home-building or -furnishing stores or specialty shops for blinds. Easy to hang, these blinds can be an attractive and cost-effective solution to making the porch inviting and comfortable at any time of day. Also to be considered are blinds that roll up or down as you see fit; these offer some measure of privacy when relaxing on the front porch.

Beautiful rustic stone columns and walls are joined by stone flooring and Arts and Crafts–style lighting fixtures on this striking front porch. A twig settee and chairs with tree-shaped cutouts are outfitted with cushions reminiscent of a mountain camp. Even the table sports a rustic twig base. Shrubs in clay pots and a basket filled with flowers are the perfect finishing touches.

Decorative Accents

Other design elements that are always a welcome addition to the front porch include a wreath dressing the front door. As a transitional area between indoors and out, what better way to offer a hearty welcome to visitors than with this lovely adornment? A grapevine wreath entwined with dried flowers is perfect for spring and summer. Think seasonal and change your wreath accordingly—perhaps one decorated with colorful dried leaves come autumn and a pine-scented balsam wreath for the winter holidays.

Pots and Planters

Accessorize the front porch with flowers planted in:

✳ Fiberglass or resin urns for classical appeal

✳ Glazed ceramic pots for a more formal look or decorative design

✳ Plastic containers that look like clay pots or simple plastic containers that can be placed inside decorative baskets

✳ Square, round, or rectangular terra-cotta pots

✳ Redwood, cedar, or cypress tubs or troughs for a rustic air

Tip: When using containers for potted flowers on the porch, include drip saucers to keep the porch floor dry and clean.

ABOVE: Even small spaces can be big on charm. This covered cottage entryway takes on porchlike appeal by introducing a metal settee and a decorative wall-hung grill. A vine-covered post and a barrel reborn as a planter make this a peaceful place to sit a spell.

OPPOSITE: Good things certainly do come in small packages, as this covered entry illustrates. A soft shade of blue on the door and house trim creates a pleasing focal point, and a casual arrangement of potted topiaries and flowers offers a smooth transition from inside to outdoors. A wooden folding chair provides a place to relax and enjoy the garden.

When it comes to decorative touches, what better place to display a flag than the front porch? The patriotic flag is always popular, but there are also purely decorative flags with nature, animal, and theme motifs that add a touch of color, beauty, or pure whimsy to the front of the house. With a bracket mounted on a porch post or column, use a wooden flagpole or painted aluminum pole that won't rust and be sure to move flags indoors during bad weather.

Another important design element for this outdoor living space is, of course, flowers. To really create that perfect outdoor room, bring a touch of the garden onto the porch by arranging containers full of colorful blooms. Place fresh flowers in a colored glass vase and set it on a table. Add clay pots or miniature urns full of geraniums on either side of the porch stairs or cluster several pots for bolder impact. If space permits, a tiered plant stand made of wood or metal can be placed against a porch wall to hold a cache of pots. And don't forget the hanging plants. Ferns (in shady spots), ivy, fuchsias, or begonias are just a few of the many plants that look wonderful in a hanging basket or container.

Last but far from least, attention to small details will ensure that your porch becomes a favorite family hangout. Games and books can be kept handy in a small trunk or table drawers, and you can have a ready supply of candles for romantic summer nights. A few choice collectibles on display will enhance the roomlike appointments of the porch and increase the comfort level—group those vintage enamelware jugs full of wildflowers, and by all means hang that vintage birdcage.

These extra little touches combined with plentiful comfortable seating add up to a room with a view the family can truly enjoy. Happy porching!

When it comes

to making the most

of an outdoor living area

and still staying within the

confines of the family budget or

space constraints, a screened or

convertible porch is a practical alter-

native to adding on a greenhouse

room or conservatory. The princi-

ples of front porch design discussed in the first

chapter can apply here, but a screened porch

can also be located at the back or side of the

house. Regardless of where it's situated, a

screened porch can be an appealing outdoor living

space from a privacy standpoint. It can also

The view from the outside is every bit as striking as the view from inside this screened porch (center porch). To take full year-round advantage of such a spectacular setting, porches are often fitted with glazed inserts as well as screens (right porch). Thus the enclosed area becomes a convertible porch that certainly ranks as the best spot in the house.

offer protection from bothersome insects and, to a certain extent, shelter from inclement weather.

Depending upon the architectural style of your home, a front porch may be outfitted with screens that fit snugly behind the balustrade or railing and between the posts and roofing. Ideally you'll want an arrangement where screens can be removed easily to take advantage of precious sunlight during the cooler months. Screens can be custom-made to fit your porch, or the ambitious do-it-yourselfer may opt to take on the challenge as a home-improvement project.

More ambitious outdoor living spaces may include converting a backyard deck into a screened room by adding a metal-framed awning and removable screened sections or by building a screened room addition to your home. Many companies offer kits for assembling screened-in living areas. Then, too, a homeowner may decide to add glazed inserts as well as screens so that the enclosed area can do double-duty as a year-round convertible porch. And no matter which route you take, quality materials and workmanship will help guarantee an outdoor space that your family will enjoy for years to come.

A winding path leads the way to this inviting screened porch. An outdoor sanctuary free of pesky insects, a screened porch also offers a measure of privacy. By carefully planning the surrounding landscape, the porch affords a colorful view and stays cool and shady, thanks to the nearby trees.

Adding Architectural Impact

Interior design for a semiopen or screened porch can get a bit more involved than dressing the open-air front porch. The type of screening material you select will affect the appearance of the room. Vinyl screening usually won't crease and can be easier for the homeowner to frame but aluminum screening has a more see-through quality that can enhance your view of the garden, the street, or whatever scenery is just beyond the porch. And if your screened porch is also fitted for custom-made windows to make it a convertible space, you'll need to determine the best type of window to use. For a project of this magnitude it's wise to consult an architect or contractor to assure optimum results, since windows are made not only in a variety of styles but with special features to reflect the sun's rays, help retain heat, and so on.

Doors are another design element to be considered. Obviously you'll have a door leading from the screened porch into the house—the front door if your porch is located in the front of the house and perhaps French

doors if your porch is just off the kitchen or family room. There is also a door (or doors) leading from the porch outside to the yard, garden, or front walk. These doors are typically screened and can be

Reminiscent of a tree house (for grown-ups), this porch combines a striking vaulted ceiling with the beauty of a wooden deck. Light and airy wicker furnishings are perfectly at home in such a natural setting, where little else is needed to create ambience. For those in a playful mood, a game is waiting nearby.

quite simple or elaborate depending upon the style of your home. Aluminum screened doors are available in different styles and colored finishes, but old-fashioned-type wooden screened doors are also made today in several styles appropriate to Victorian architectural designs, farmhouses, cottages, and bungalows.

What next? Well, what about the walls of the screened porch? This may not be a big concern if the porch is an enclosed space off the exterior of the house. In that case, the façade creates a wall of rustic cedar shakes, brick, stone, clapboard, siding, or painted shingles. In contrast, if this outdoor living area is planned as an addition to the house (especially when fitted with windows for year-round use), the wall treatment becomes an important concern and a strong decorative element. Depending upon your personal style and taste, walls can be paneled with plain wood or beadboard, painted, or dressed with wallpaper. Regarding wallpaper, keep in mind that a vinyl wall covering will be easy to clean. Also, many wallpaper patterns have coordinating fabrics that can be ideal for making tablecloths, chair cushions, throw pillows, or window treatments for a more traditional approach to decorating an outdoor living space.

When it comes to flooring, the screened porch built from scratch can incorporate pressure-treated lumber installed deck fashion, tongue-and-groove planks, or hardwood flooring. A wood floor can be stained or painted, and depending upon the decorative style of your screened or convertible porch, you may want to consider a special paint technique. Spattering small flecks of color across a painted wood floor can be ideal in a country setting, while creating a checkerboard effect would complement either a country or a traditional decor. Deck flooring can be enhanced with a room-size weather-treated carpet or sisal matting—something to help prevent bugs and insects from venturing "indoors."

Other flooring possibilities for the screened porch include the masonry variety—slate, tile, brick, or concrete. Slate is easy to care for and an ideal floor treatment in a casual setting. Quarry tile, often referred to as terra-cotta tile because of its familiar red-brown hues, is also available in shades of rose or gray. Quarry tiles can be found in many different sizes and shapes so they offer numerous possibilities for designing a unique floor. Yet another member of the masonry family, brick, is especially at home in a rustic outdoor living space because of its rugged texture and strong, natural appeal. Bricks can be used to create a variety of decorative patterns, such as the ever-popular herringbone design. Like slate, brick flooring should be sealed to prevent stains. Finally, for some homeowners concrete flooring may be a practical alternative to other flooring options, or perhaps an existing concrete patio is being converted to a screened porch. Either way, concrete can always be painted to create a decorative effect or covered with an indoor-outdoor carpet to provide a bit of cushioning underfoot.

Decor

The screened or convertible porch is similar to the open-air front porch in that you'll want to consider its decor carefully. But while the front porch itself often serves as the focal point of the exterior of the home (with furnishings being decorative accessories), a screened porch can call for more extensive planning in regard to function, color scheme, decorative style, furnishings, accessories, and focal points. In other words, you should approach decorating this stylish outdoor space just as you would any other room in the home.

Since the screened porch is a casual, carefree space where you can serve meals, entertain, or simply relax and enjoy solitude, it may be furnished and outfitted to accommodate several activities or just one or two. Determine exactly what role you want the screened porch to play and the mood you wish to create—then take it from there.

Keeping the screened porch light and airy generally means calling upon a white, neutral, or pastel color scheme and then perhaps using bolder colors for playful accents. Or go for the red, yellow, and blue scheme, with just a dash of green or orange. Bright primary and secondary colors have a way of giving a casual room a cheerful, laid-back feeling. If, on the other hand, you're decorating a porch on a log home or a woodland cottage, a rustic design may call for earth tones or a deep forest green color scheme. The architectural style and location of your home can help determine the color palette. Keep in mind that light colors can make a small space appear larger while deep shades can cozy up a large expanse. Depending upon your personal style, perhaps a compromise is called for. The perfect example would be a screened or convertible porch with a striking white backdrop and a beautiful pine-finished beadboard ceiling.

What's your preference in regard to style? Do you adore the English cottage look or are you drawn to American country? Are you perhaps most comfortable in an eclectic or contemporary setting? Traditional European designs and nineteenth-century Victoriana have a great deal of charm, as do whimsical retro looks. No matter what your taste when it comes to interior design, the screened porch can be the perfect spot to highlight the casual or playful side of your favorite design scheme.

A nautical theme makes a personal statement on this inviting screened porch. Stone flooring inlaid with a brass "compass" and the white wood-beamed ceiling and trim blend effortlessly with the exterior shingles that create a natural backdrop. A built-in seat with storage compartments keeps clutter at bay and offers a relaxing spot for catnaps. White wicker furnishings with jaunty blue and white striped cushions lend a decorative and coordinated touch. Subtle hints of yellow—in the checkered lamp shade, throw pillows, and bouquet of sunflowers—add a pleasing contrast.

Casual Chairs and Occasional Tables

Furnishing the screened porch can be as much fun as enjoying the room itself. While you can certainly visit designer showrooms and fine home-furnishing stores if you so desire, keep in mind that second-hand tables, antique wicker chairs, and vintage fabrics for cushions and pillows can all turn up at flea markets, yard sales, antiques shows, and auctions. Make a list of your needs and start hunting! That old weathered table you might come across can be given a new lease on life with a fresh coat of paint; the old bench spotted at a flea market would be ideal for stacking books or games . . . you get the idea. You don't need to spend a small fortune to create a comfortable, inviting, and stylish outdoor living space.

Generally when we think about screened porch furnishings we conjure up images of wicker rockers, a large wooden table, or perhaps a wrought-iron settee piled high with comfy cushions. There are no hard and fast rules when it comes to filling this casual space, so mix and match to fashion your own rendition of the perfect outdoor living room while keeping a few key points in mind.

If you're considering antique wicker furniture for the screened porch, there

A Texas landscape can be thoroughly enjoyed from this rustic screened porch. Comfortable wicker chairs pull up to a large round table for relaxed meals no matter what the weather. Screens have been designed to attach to the porch frame in front of the railing system and are no doubt favored for comfort during the hot summer months but can be removed in cooler weather.

Sunday Brunch with the Family

✳ A wonderful platter full of warm breads, muffins, and coffee cakes can accompany scrambled eggs and ham, French toast, quiche, or the house specialty.

✳ Dress the porch table in a lovely lace or linen tablecloth and matching napkins.

✳ Dust off the good china and silverware and set the table.

✳ Arrange a low bouquet of flowers in a cut-glass vase as a centerpiece.

are several styles available. During the late 1800s many pieces (made with hardwood frames and rattan, reed, or cane) were crafted with ornate curlicues and decorative embellishments typical of the Victorian age. As the stylistic excess of the era gave way to simplified furnishings, wicker with open latticework designs became popular during the early 1900s, especially at resort hotels. Then, too, cushioned wicker furnishings designed with a close-weave pattern were introduced during the Arts and Crafts period between 1910 and 1920. Finally, machine-made wicker furnishings constructed of a strong paper fiber on the Lloyd loom became widely available by the early 1920s and were accessorized with bright chintz cushions. Sporting a square or boxy shape, these wicker pieces were intended for indoor use only.

Examine antique wicker for sound construction and good condition. Vintage pieces can always be painted for a fresh look unless they wear an original varnish over the natural tone. These "natural" pieces are at the high-cost end of the market, and painting over a natural finish would significantly decrease the value of the piece. An old wicker piece with extensive damage can be costly to repair. If restoration work is needed to replace missing pieces of wicker or other damage, seek the services of a professional.

Exactly what's out there that won't cost a small fortune? Visit large antiques shows and you're certain to come across vintage wicker chairs and rockers, tables, planters, and child-size chairs and rockers. You should be able to assemble an eye-catching and comfortable assortment of pieces ideal for a screened porch with a casual country, Victorian, eclectic, traditional, or even rustic decorating scheme. And for the homeowner whose taste is definitely modern, furniture manufacturers are turning out wicker in contemporary styles and mail-order catalogs are offering everything from chic European designs to pieces with simple, clean lines.

Wood furnishings for a screened or convertible porch can be rustic, reminiscent of a specific decorative period, or contemporary. For casual family meals or entertaining, an old pine harvest table will work nicely, as will a picnic table decked out with a colorful tablecloth. This venerable favorite is just as

appropriate on the porch as it is in the backyard. Depending upon the configuration of available space, choose a rectangular or round table with sturdy benches that can be accessorized with plump cushions. And while a natural wood finish or a stained finish on a table may be preferred, a picnic table can always be given a colorful coat of enamel paint.

Assorted wooden chairs, rockers, or a settee can be introduced to create a relaxing conversation area, and it is important to make sure you have an adequate number of small tables close by for books, refreshments, and so on. Contemporary wooden furnishings for an outdoor living space have crisp, clean lines, while rustic twig items made of willow or hickory have definite camp-style or rustic appeal. Vintage twig pieces can be found through antiques dealers that specialize in camp accessories, and modern renditions are being crafted by skilled artisans as well as by notable furniture manufacturers. Other wooden furnishings have garden appeal, such as the cedar chairs and settees crafted for English-style gardens.

Metal furnishings—such as a glass-topped table with a metal base and an assortment of chairs—can be quite striking when given a coat of white, black, or dark green paint. To provide maximum comfort when dining, make sure chairs are outfitted with plump cushions so that guests will be content to linger and converse over coffee. New metal furnishings are available in a wide array of designs and colored finishes, or you can opt for a retro look and assemble a collection of those metal "motel"

ABOVE: Perfect for casual or elegant meals, this screened porch accommodates a table that comfortably seats four. Careful attention to detail makes this outdoor living area every bit as inviting as the indoors. A cheerful floral print tablecloth plays host to a lovely table setting, where simple bouquets make a fitting centerpiece and a medley of chair styles seems completely at home.

OPPOSITE: The beauty of the wood-finished flooring and ceiling of this screened porch are complemented by simple wicker and metal furnishings. Shade-loving flowers and plants are thoughtfully arranged in containers, and breakfast is served with a breathtaking view.

chairs that were so popular during the 1930s and 1940s. These, too, can be made more inviting with colorful cushions.

Regardless of what type of furniture you select for the screened or convertible porch, the key to casual comfort is easy maintenance and carefree design. Save the upholstered sofa for the family room and go with the cushioned glider instead. Add comfortable chairs with cushions made of easy-care fabrics such as canvas, duck, sailcloth, or ticking. Chintz can always be used for inviting toss pillows.

Regarding furnishings, there's one other thing to keep in mind. Like any other room in your home, the screened porch should have a focal point. In many cases it may be the view, but then again we don't all live on a lake or enjoy majestic mountain scenery. Not to worry—an eye-catching arrangement of furniture can become a focal point, or something as simple as a timeworn table sporting a bouquet of fresh flowers can draw the eye in an outdoor living space.

To control natural lighting on the screened porch, nonfabric shades are practical and in keeping with a casual decorating scheme. Along with matchstick and bamboo shades, shades made of woven grasses and woven wood are also available. If your porch is fitted with windows for year-round use, consider rice-paper shades or lovely fabric Roman shades with insulating properties and a sun guard to prevent fading. Vertical and horizontal blinds made of vinyl, wood, and metal come in myriad colors, but keep in mind that a minimal window treatment is important to avoid losing the outdoor appeal of a screened room.

For a dressy effect on a screened or convertible porch—perhaps with an English country decorating scheme—window valances or swags can be made from a sturdy fabric such as canvas and then embellished with colorful trim and hung on striking metal rods. Just be sure to use a weather-resistant fabric or something relatively inexpensive like patterned bed sheets, which don't involve a sizable investment.

Lighting the screened porch calls for a generous supply of candles for creating ambience during relaxing evening hours. General and task lighting will also be required for entertaining and quieter pursuits such as reading or hobby work. Recessed lighting or a ceiling fixture—even an informal chandelier—can

Container Gardening

Shade-loving plants for clay pots, window boxes, and other containers on the screened porch include:

* Begonia
* Boston fern
* Coleus
* English ivy
* Fuchsia
* Hosta
* Impatiens

The epitome of the ideal outdoor retreat, this screened porch has both country flair and sophisticated touches. A beautiful woodland backdrop plays host to a porch designed with a tongue-and-groove ceiling, a wooden floor painted to resemble a room-size rug, and a decorative drapery treatment. Wicker furnishings happily coexist with a tiny rustic twig table and an elegant round table for intimate meals. An abundance of flowers and plants brings nature onto the porch.

provide allover illumination, and a table lamp or two will serve perfectly for tasks. Wicker, metal, or pottery-based lamps with solid or patterned fabric shades are strong possibilities. You can also have lamps made from odd items such as an old stoneware jug or a vintage watering can—the perfect addition to an outdoor room. And don't forget the ceiling fan, which can, of course, include lights. Fans are made in so many styles and colors that your choices are almost limitless. Especially advantageous on a screened porch for cooling and air circulation, a fan can have strong decorative impact.

Other design elements will enhance the personal aspect of your screened porch. You say you love baskets? Baskets are ideal on the porch for flowers and for holding books, toys, and so on. You like the look of metal? Galvanized French flower pails are perfect for displaying bouquets of wildflowers or fresh cuttings from the garden. And how about that collection of vintage enamelware you've got in the kitchen? Old enameled containers such as buckets, pitchers, and even coffeepots are great for housing flowers and plants.

It's important to bring the outdoors onto the porch so that one area flows effortlessly into another. Fresh flowers, potted plants, and hanging baskets will fill the screened porch with outdoor spirit. If space allows, consider a wooden or wire plant stand to group pots of flowers together for strong visual impact. Wall hangings might include framed botanical prints or seed packets. It's simply a matter of putting your imagination to work.

Finishing decorative touches for a screened or convertible porch should be spirited. Restraint is important, however, so that you don't clutter up what should be an airy, open space. Flooring can be accessorized with colorful area rugs, playful hooked rugs, or summery sisal matting. Think stripes, checks, and bright floral patterns. Even sisal matting, highly durable and woven of plant fibers, can be embellished with stenciled designs or colored trim.

Take a good look around your screened porch and use a critical eye. What will make it more comfortable or inviting? How about a lovely fabric or lace tablecloth, a lavender wreath hanging on the wall, or a picture frame made with seashells? Decorating around a theme is fun, too. A nautical motif might call for old oars hung high on the wall. The nature lover might find pleasure in adding a collection of rustic decoys, birdhouses, or fishing creels. Whatever your interests, introduce select pieces into the porch decor and you will have created not only a personal haven but a room to be enjoyed by one and all.

Screened porches are ideal for alfresco dining, since the screening keeps hungry insects away while allowing refreshing breezes in. This porch has been outfitted in a playful mix of styles, from the sleek elegance of the glass table to the retro charm of the vintage vinyl dinette chairs.

The backyard deck affords unlimited options when it comes to creating stylish living spaces outside. Modern deck designs can be virtually any shape or size, have multiple levels for dif- 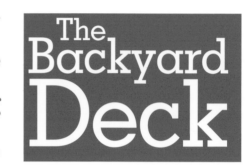 ferent activities, and incorporate everything from built-in seating and planters to decorative finishes that make the deck an attractive asset to your home. Planning is all-important when it comes to building a deck. Not only do you want it to expand your living space but you usually must consider access to the house, the architectural features of your home, and landscaping around

A striking arched doorway frames the perfect view available from the deck, which is just off the kitchen. The surrounding scenery can be enjoyed and casual meals shared from comfortable wicker chairs. Weather-resistant striped seat cushions are perfect for a relaxed outdoor setting, and with the addition of a lovely tablecloth and bouquet of flowers, this becomes a favorite place to sip drinks or dine under the bright blue sky.

the deck. Unless you hire an architect, designer, or contractor to work up layouts, you'll want to do some drawings or sketches to get ideas down on paper. Home-building centers have deck packages available in assorted sizes for standard rectangular or square decks. As with any building project, check your local building and zoning laws before you begin.

While selecting lumber to construct a deck may seem a purely practical consideration, it's actually an important design element. Different woods have different looks and develop varying patinas if left to weather naturally. Redwood is an excellent choice for a deck thanks to the wood's durability and natural beauty. If left untreated it will weather to a silvery gray, or it can be stained to retain its rich, reddish coloring.

Cypress and cedar have a rougher texture well suited to a rustic vacation cabin or woodland home. Either can be stained or left natural and will stand up to the elements as well as redwood will, but both are generally less expensive. Then, too, there's always pressure-treated lumber, which has somewhat of a greenish tint from the chemicals used to treat the wood. This green tint will eventually fade and the wood will weather to a soft gray. Pressure-treated lumber is quite strong and a favorite for deck building in the northern United States, where #1 yellow pine (a specific grade of pressure-treated lumber) is certainly more cost-effective than redwood. In contrast, the relative availability of redwood in the western states makes that particular material more competitive price-wise in that region.

To ensure that the deck you build will last for many years to come, it should be soundly constructed with one of the woods mentioned above and stainless-steel or hot-dipped galvanized nails and fasteners. A penetrating finish with a water repellent or a deck stain that contains a water repellent should be used. Such a finish is applied annually or at least every few years to extend the life of a deck. Other deck-preserving measures include sweeping it quite regularly and cleaning between the boards with a special tool available at home-building centers. These procedures prevent organic material from accumulating in crevices, which would increase the risk of wood rot. Power washing or using a deck-washing solution every one to two years will also help keep your deck in top shape.

Front and center, open decking is outfitted with casual, move-anywhere sling-back canvas chairs. A covered porch is located on the side of this vacation home, for those times when shelter from rain or from too much sun is welcome. Situating the porch on the side rather than the front keeps the view unobstructed and makes the most of natural lighting.

Creating Privacy

Once your deck has been built or an existing deck has been refurbished, expanded, or repaired, it's time to consider how best to outfit this open-air extension of your home. For maximum comfort and enjoyment, consider whether or not privacy is an issue. If you live in a rural area you may want as little as possible hindering the view from your deck, but many homeowners want to create a visual barrier between their outdoor living space and that of the next-door neighbor. Lattice panels, fencing, decorative railings, planters, and shrubs can all provide privacy. Lattice panels can be cut to any size and framed with pressure-treated lumber or posts to enclose the entire deck or simply to create a privacy screen for a certain area.

Lattice is also an inexpensive way of achieving a dressy or decorative effect in an outdoor living space. Panels can be stained or painted to match the decking and, once positioned, can even serve as a trellis for climbing vines and plants. Lattice is ideal for enclosing space devoted to a hot tub or spa as well as an area devoted to outdoor meals. Often used as deck or porch skirting, lattice can also provide some measure of shade throughout the day when used in an overhead structure or sun shelter on a deck. It allows air to circulate freely while blocking out some of the sun's rays, and you can train climbing vines to grow across it to create a sort of natural ceiling where deep shade is desired.

OPPOSITE: Truly an outdoor living room, this spacious deck has been outfitted with a lattice roof to provide a measure of shade. The dark green wicker set, accessorized with summery striped cushions, even includes two couches—ideal for drowsing on a warm summer afternoon. Pots and bouquets of flowers, candles, and a bowl of fresh fruit lend warmth and inviting charm to the setting.

ABOVE, LEFT: A gray painted deck, which coordinates nicely with the siding, is enhanced with built-in planters, benches, and angular privacy screens. Introducing these decorative measures not only makes additional seating available, but allows the deck to take on room-like proportions and qualities. The raised floral beds become an eye-catching backdrop.

ABOVE, RIGHT: This large deck is enclosed by a decorative railing that sports a crisscross design and a privacy screen at the far end. Pressure-treated lumber has been allowed to weather to a natural, soft gray while the bright red posts add a dash of color. Lightweight director's chairs can easily be moved to take advantage of sun or shade.

Fencing and railings can also be used to enhance an outdoor living area. When incorporated as a part of your deck design, keep in mind that a solid wall of fencing will cut down on breezes and air circulation. To maintain an open and spacious setting, consider fencing that has spaces between the slats or fencing with a latticework top. There are so many styles available through specialty shops, home-building centers, and lumber yards that you should have no problem finding a fence design to complement your deck. You can stain fencing to match the deck or allow it to weather naturally. Be sure to check local ordinances for height restrictions.

ABOVE, LEFT: The honey-colored built-in planter that runs the length of this backyard deck adds visual interest and natural beauty, and creates a private spot for sunbathing or exercising. Not only does the planter allow the flower bed free rein, but the overhead trellis offers space for hanging plants and climbing vines such as morning glories.

ABOVE, RIGHT: A close-up of this weathered deck showcases the planters that are arranged in a tiered design. Petunias and marigolds add vivid color to the natural surroundings and become a pleasing focal point.

OPPOSITE: A weathered deck with an elaborate railing that almost acts as a fence makes an ideal outdoor living space when outfitted with rattan furnishings and an artistic metal side table. Small but significant touches, such as the blue and white throw pillow and the vase filled with bird-of-paradise, add homey comfort.

From a safety standpoint as well as a decorative one, you may opt instead for a notable railing that also provides some measure of privacy. A series of horizontal wood slats with flat-topped posts makes a sturdy railing and even provides space to set potted plants. For something more traditional, there are numerous spindle styles to choose from when designing a railing.

Large wooden planters built into your deck can also help create privacy. Visit the local library and thumb through how-to books to find practical ideas and step-by-step instructions. Use planters at one end of the deck or locate them between built-in benches. Planters can also be purely decorative when placed alongside steps leading up to the deck. For those who'd rather not tackle a building project, plants can still be used for privacy by placing ivy or other climbers in lightweight pots with a trellis attached and positioning them on the deck where needed to create a natural screen.

Regarding landscaping, since the deck is a casual and informal extension of your home, natural hedges are preferrable to a formal, clipped hedgerow when it comes to planting shrubs for privacy. Barberry is a wonderful example of a hedge that will grow quickly and enhance the area surrounding a deck.

Crisp, clean lines in the railings and columns are the ideal backdrop for simple wicker furnishings with an outdoorsy green trim. A commanding view takes center stage, so decorative accessories are kept to a minimum—a potted dwarf tree and a planter filled with vibrant yellow blooms are enough. There can't possibly be a better spot to enjoy sweet summer fruits and a refreshing glass of iced tea.

To really make full use of a backyard deck and the private or social activities that take place there, a combination of sunny and shaded areas offers the best of both worlds. For the deck bathed in sunlight, immediate solutions include a large, freestanding umbrella that can be positioned where needed, a table with a center umbrella, or a canvas awning. Awnings, whether retractable or stationary, provide not only relief from the sun but shelter from raindrops, which can come in handy when dining outdoors. A long-term solution for creating shade involves landscaping. Plant shade trees nearby so that in a few years' time a portion of the deck will have constant shade from a small and lovely flowering crabapple or a larger red maple tree.

With the help of a few design elements that enhance a relaxed setting, the deck can still be the most popular place for the family to gather even after the sun sets. Stargazing under cover of darkness can be a pleasant pastime but mood lighting can bring the deck to life during the evening hours. An outdoor fixture attached to the exterior of the house near the door assures safe entry and exit from the deck. The soft lighting of a low-voltage bulb is generally more attractive than a bright light for this purpose.

This backyard deck is a garden-inspired haven perfect for a small country cottage. Landscaping with flowers, trees, and climbing vines transforms the deck into an oasis of natural beauty. The table is accessorized with a color-coordinated sun umbrella and seashell-patterned linens. The blue and white color palette extends to small details such as the chair cushions, the dishes, and the petite checkered shades on the candlestick lamps.

Landscape lights around the perimeter of the deck cast a subtle glow that can filter light onto the deck during the evening. Consider mushroom or tier lights that provide low-level lighting and actually serve as a design accent. There are also well lights that can be positioned in the nearby landscape to cast a beam of light upward, either toward the deck or into nearby trees or a garden area close by. Then, too, small twinkle lights can be strung on a deck railing or on a deck umbrella to provide subtle lighting and ambience. And as always, candlelight can be ideal in an outdoor living space to set a relaxing, intimate tone. Beautiful spear-tip lanterns that hold long-burning votives can be placed in the yard around the deck, and citronella candles in colored glass or pottery dishes can be placed on tabletops to help keep pesky insects at bay. Freestanding kerosene lanterns in a beautiful array of finishes are also available for lighting the deck.

Hammocks and Picnic Tables

Without a doubt, furnishings are the most important element of a stylish deck and usually become the focal point. Unless you have an assortment of furniture pieces to meet your needs, the deck will just be an area that is passed through on the way into the house. Consider what the deck will be used for and shop accordingly. Do you need a table and chairs for casual meals? What about a place to really relax and unwind—would a hammock fill the bill? Or perhaps a chaise longue? For entertaining, do you need an assortment of chairs that are lightweight and easy to move? And what about the family budget? Make a list of what's needed, decide how much you'd like to spend, and consider all of the following options. Keep in mind that you'll want furniture that's weather-resistant and a snap to take care of.

Wooden furniture is ideal on the deck where it blends beautifully with the texture of this outdoor space. Cedar, redwood, teak, and pressure-treated lumber are all used to make outdoor furnishings that will withstand the elements. Traditional and contemporary designs can be found through furniture manufacturers, mail-order specialty catalogs, design studios, garden shops, home-building centers, and regional artisans. Everything from sturdy Adirondack chairs and modern pieces to English garden settees and rustic tables are available. Individual pieces at home on the deck include chairs, rockers, settees, tables, benches, swings, and recliners or chaise longues. Wooden furnishings can be painted, stained, or left to weather to a soft silvery gray. Remember that colorful cushions will

Taking advantage of the lovely view, this deck was designed and constructed to accommodate a large shade tree that just happens to serve as a support for a beautiful hammock. Weathered to a subtle silvery gray, the deck overlooks a small brook and is accessorized with a small potted tree and plant. The hammock is made more inviting with colorful toss pillows and a warm throw for cool afternoons.

make furnishings much more comfortable and inviting, so look for fabrics such as weather-resistant synthetics or vinyls in striped, checkered, or floral designs. If there's a downside to using wooden furniture on the deck it's the fact that wood tends to be heavy, so it can be a chore to move items from place to place.

When it comes to metal furniture, forget about those simple folding chairs with webbed-tape seats and explore what's new in the world of aluminum. Outdoor furnishings with aluminum frames are available in a vast array of colored finishes and are generally scratch- and weather-resistant. Tape, mesh, cushioned, and molded metal chair seats and backs allow for diversity in seating choices with modern, period, and European designs. A beautiful glass-topped table with eye-catching aluminum chairs can make a striking focal point on the deck. Aluminum also has the advantage of being lightweight, so if you do tend to rearrange furniture on the deck regularly, these furnishings won't cause any backaches.

Yet another choice when it comes to outfitting the deck is resin furniture. Available just about anywhere, resin tables, chairs, loungers, rockers, and multipositional chairs are a cost-effective way to furnish the deck on a budget. These weather-resistant furnishings come in a variety of colors including white, green, and red—usually with a high-gloss finish—and they're easy to maintain. Since they resist dirt, stains, and mildew, a little soap and water is all it takes to make them as good as new. It is also worth noting that there are specialty manufacturers that produce resin outdoor furniture with the old-fashioned good looks of wicker. Much more costly than the chain-store variety, these resin pieces

Sunny yellow paint gives this deck a festive air, and by adding a medley of colors on the picnic set, a rainbow effect is achieved. Paint is always an affordable way of creating an eye-catching, decorative backdrop or focal point.

A weathered Adirondack chair is pulled up to the edge of this sun-bleached deck to take full advantage of fresh breezes and a coastal view. The beauty of the natural terrain is repeated in an aged wooden barrel filled with tall grasses.

are beautiful and impervious to the weather and make a stunning focal point on the backyard deck, where their natural-looking finish adds a nice bit of texture.

Once your backyard deck is furnished, what do you add in the way of accoutrements and decorative accessories? Since the backyard living space has long been associated with cookouts and barbecues, a grill is a necessity if you enjoy cooking and entertaining outdoors. It's strictly a matter of personal preference whether you opt for a charcoal or gas grill. There are advantages to each and grills range from the plain and simple to state-of-the-art. Generally, if you're interested in a portable grill that gives food a noticeable smoky flavor, a charcoal model is for you. Charcoal grills require preparation time for coals to develop adequate heat, but devoted fans insist the wait is worth it. In contrast, a gas grill can include several convenient features, involves less start-up time, and has evenly distributed heat. A gas grill is more costly than a charcoal model and propane tanks need to be refilled. Whatever type of grill you decide to invest in, a durable cover is a good idea when the grill is not in use. You may also

The ultimate outdoor luxury or accessory, a hot tub is ideally suited to a backyard deck. This inviting retreat offers outdoor ambience with shelter from the elements and curtains that add instant privacy. Pillows for lounging, towels for drying off, and candlelight for atmosphere are joined by a trio of— what else—rubber ducks!

want to consider a decorative L-shaped panel trellis to hide the grill from plain sight. Easy to move, such an accessory can also be used to partition off a work area for gardening supplies, toys, or the like.

As an open-air room the deck should be easy to move around in, so overcrowding with furnishings is certainly to be avoided. Introduce what is necessary in the way of furniture and then keep folding chairs ready for larger crowds. Plan a color scheme and use that to select chair cushions. When used year after year cushions can begin to look tired, so change your color scheme and redecorate every few years to give the deck a face-lift. If you've grown immune to the charms of that green and white striped fabric, by all means try cushions with a floral design or a vibrant solid color.

Hot off the Grill

✳ Plan an outdoor barbecue for early fall—it will be appreciated even more because the summer picnic season seems so distant.

✳ Grill a variety of seasonal vegetables fresh from a nearby farmer's market or produce store and serve along with your favorite barbecue foods. Late corn, tomatoes, and all kinds of squash are wonderful when grilled.

✳ Use easy-care graniteware dishes that are a snap to clean and won't break if dropped.

✳ Fill a colored glass bottle or jar with wildflowers and use it as a centerpiece.

✳ Protect foods from insects with mesh dome covers that fit nicely over serving dishes and are available in assorted sizes.

✳ Have cold salads and dessert prepared ahead of time so you can relax and enjoy your guests—and your backyard deck.

This tiled area is outfitted for serious outdoor pleasure and culinary delights. Not only does it include a brick hearth for chilly evenings, but a complete outdoor kitchen has been designed for convenience and enjoyment. Everything needed to prepare a meal— mini refrigerator, sink, oven, grill, and storage space—is at hand. Dinner is served at the wooden table, which is surrounded by English-style garden chairs that are cushioned for comfort.

A Garden of Pots and Planters

What about other decorative accessories for the deck? By far the most versatile and beautiful are flowers and verdant plants. The deck is a wonderful spot for containers full of blooms, herbs, vegetables, or even small trees or topiaries. Consider your approach to decorating the backyard deck. What's your style? Select containers according to what blends beautifully with a modern setting (such as plain clay or concrete planters) or a traditional decor (such as small urns or painted wooden containers). If you've decided on a garden or cottage-style theme, look to clay pots embellished with molded designs or colorful glazed ceramic pots or jardinieres. There are also fiberglass containers that

look like stone or terra-cotta but with a fraction of the weight. Less expensive containers made of plastic come in a variety of colors and styles, and some plastic pots look like clay. If the thought of plastic leaves you cold, remember that you can always set plastic containers inside beautiful baskets.

Other containers for use on the backyard deck include recycled objects you may have about the house or unusual items you come across at flea markets. Almost anything can find new life as an eye-catching flowerpot—a vintage watering can, decorative product tins, old wire baskets lined with moss, or wicker baskets with plastic liners. Check your local nursery and gardening catalogs for attractive trivets, saucers, decorative wooden platforms on casters, and molded clay "feet" that come in handy for raising containers off the deck surface. Elevating pots and containers makes for healthier plants by providing air circulation and is a surefire way to avoid unsightly water stains on the deck.

As far as container planting is concerned, the deck is ideally suited to annuals with colorful foliage or beautiful blooms that will be long-lasting or repeat throughout the season. You can plant from seed come early spring or wait a bit and visit the local nursery to select plants. Keep your deck's location

A cluster of decorative terra-cotta planters filled with vibrant petunias adds a burst of color to the arid landscape that surrounds this deck. The group of planters creates a much stronger visual impact than if the pots were scattered along the deck.

in mind when choosing annuals to make up your container "gardens." Is the deck generally sunny or shady, or does it offer both? Most plants at the nursery include information on the appropriate exposure for best results. You'll also want to think about those plants that do well in your particular region of the country. With this in mind, it's interesting to note that some perennials, such as petunias, geraniums, and coleus, are actually sold as annuals depending upon the climate.

Use your decorator's eye when selecting flowers and foliage for the deck. Keep your color scheme in mind—use a lead color and perhaps two accent colors. For example, red geraniums are beautiful but perhaps even more so when joined by a handful of white or pink flowers for heightened interest. Or concentrate on a single color and plant containers with several variations of that particular shade. You can also create strong focus or visual impact on the deck by planting different flowers of the same color. Designing containers calls for planning—you'll want to blend a foundation plant (perhaps something with some height) with flowers and an ivy or some other cascading plant to create a pleasing arrangement.

Perennials and shrubs can also be planted in containers to serve as visual anchors on the deck, provided that you don't live in an area with severe winters. Check at the local nursery to find out which perennials will do best in a pot and what shrubs tend to grow slowly—otherwise you'll be repotting before you know it. Other possibilities for container gardening on the deck include cacti, miniature roses, herbs, dwarf vegetables, and strawberries.

To show containers at their best advantage, cluster flowerpots in certain areas of your deck to help define space. Situate an arrangement of terra-cotta pots filled with vibrant blooms near a table and chairs to enhance alfresco meals. Or line up several attractive containers on a bench for a pleasing view. Use

---

Summertime Flowers

Annuals that are ideal for deck pots and containers include:

* Forget-me-not
* Impatiens
* Lobelia
* Marigold
* Nasturtium
* Phlox
* Primrose
* Sweet alyssum
* Sweet pea

Perennials often grown as annuals include:

* Begonia
* Coleus
* Dusty miller
* Fuchsia
* Geranium
* Pansy
* Petunia

containers on deck stairs to spotlight the way to your outdoor living area. The possibilities are endless, and just as you can change your gardening color scheme from year to year, so too can you play with the location of pots.

Other decorative elements that might be added to a backyard deck include metal, wicker, or wire plant stands to cluster plants at different heights, a trellis placed against the house and covered with ivy or colorful morning glories, a birdbath to invite backyard residents up close, wind chimes to help enjoy a soft breeze, and even miniature water gardens such as tabletop fountains or small plastic ponds that can easily be moved about.

Acting as a footbridge to the handsome French doors of the house, this deck also serves as a relaxing spot to enjoy the beauty of the natural surroundings. Metal handrails have been combined with vintage wooden posts for a unique and charming look, while the urns serving as planters reinforce the "antiques" theme. A small table sporting a sun umbrella creates a perfect place for enjoying the view, and the sling-back chair invites curling up with a good book.

As a combination recreation and relaxation space, the poolside patio can be the most popular seasonal or year-round area of your home. While the pool may indeed be the focal point, the patio can display stunning beauty all its own.  You have several attractive and decorative options when it comes to designing and building a patio, and each should be considered in terms of stylish effect, durability, and cost.

The majority of patios are fashioned from brick, stone, concrete, or tile. Patio bricks or pavers are available in a variety of colors and textures and are graded according to climate.

This idyllic backyard retreat has it all—attractive fencing for privacy and safety, an inviting pool for laps or lazy splashing, and a stone patio for sunbathing, barbecuing, and alfresco dining. A trio of flower-filled pots flanks each end of the pool for decorative impact.

Anyone living in a northern area should invest in "severe weather" bricks that can withstand sub-freezing temperatures and freeze-thaw weather cycles. Usually set in sand or concrete, bricks are virtually maintenance-free and can be arranged in any number of eye-catching designs such as diagonal, herringbone, or basketweave, or a simple running pattern. In terms of creating style, brick is very versatile; depending upon the pattern you select when laying bricks down, the patio can have a traditional air, modern appeal, or old-fashioned rustic charm.

Stone patios are usually formed from flagstone (a thin, irregularly sized stone), rubble or round pebbles, or ashlar (a square-cut stone of uniform depth or thickness). From a design standpoint a stone patio can be quite elegant. Flagstone has a time-honored classic appeal, while rubble and ashlar are ideal in a contemporary setting. Each is available in a variety of colors to match any decorating scheme. Like brick, stone can be set in sand, but using a concrete base or mortar will help guarantee that a patio will last for years.

There's no doubt that a stylish patio can be achieved using brick or stone, but what about concrete? Simply put, a concrete patio doesn't have to

Custom-crafted pools can be built in a variety of shapes.
Designed to fit the landscape and take full advantage of
the mountain view, this pool is surrounded by
a half-moon stone patio, where chaise longues face
the lovely scenery. Portable sun umbrellas create
instant shade wherever it's desired.

be dull and boring. You can dress it up by adding tiny pebbles or hints of color to poured concrete or it can be "finished" with a special trowel that adds texture. Even a push broom can be dragged across wet concrete to create a wavy or checkered pattern. For a small patio, concrete may be a less expensive alternative to other options, but for a large area you should certainly compare costs.

Another possibility when it comes to designing a poolside patio is tile. Especially popular in warm climates, tiles are available as pavers, in mosaic form, or as large quarry tiles. For European flair consider mosaic for the patio, or choose quarry tiles for a vintage, old-world style. Pavers can also be used to create any number of colorful and decorative designs, from high style to simply casual. Just be certain that the tile you select has a rough or uneven surface texture so that it won't become dangerously slippery when wet.

ABOVE, LEFT: Terra-cotta tiles, perfect in a warm climate, make a stunning poolside patio. A decorative tile planter, color-coordinated to match the tiles in the pool and filled with blooms and trellises, runs the length of the house. A pair of comfortable chaise longues sit front and center with a whimsical folk-art alligator table between them. Note, too, the dining area placed under cover in the background and the select use of planters for adding greenery.

ABOVE, RIGHT: Here, terra-cotta tiles are set in graceful scallops, a pattern favored in classical Italian courtyards.

OPPOSITE: This large, multifunctional outdoor area makes wonderful use of available space. A custom-designed pool is surrounded by a raised garden bed, which is made of brick and filled with shrubs. The spacious stone patio allows the owner to arrange wooden furnishings into several groupings, while a covered section with tile flooring is reserved for casual meals.

Ideally, the patio serves both as a gateway to the pool and as an extended outdoor living area. You'll want it to be large enough to accommodate several chairs or chaise longues for sunbathing and a table and chairs for outdoor meals and poolside refreshments. Naturally the patio design is influenced by the type, size, and shape of the pool in the backyard. When giving thought to a swimming pool and patio,

you should put your ideas on paper so that you'll have some sense of the space that can be devoted to the patio, area, landscaping, flower beds, storage area, and so on.

As the focal point of the backyard setting, a pool can involve considerable investment. There are different types available, and you'll want to consider the various options as well as the impact on your family budget. Aboveground pools with frames of steel, aluminum, or polymer resin are sold in various sizes in round, rectangular, or oblong shapes and depths of four or five feet (1.2m or 1.5m). For the family on a tight budget or with a particularly limited amount of space, an aboveground pool can be enhanced

---

ABOVE, LEFT: The old stone façade of this beautiful home no doubt inspired the use of stone for the patio and pool edging. A landscape design combining trees, shrubs, and flowers creates privacy and provides natural color and texture. A wooden chaise longue outfitted with a cheerful blue and white striped cushion is the best seat in the house.

ABOVE, RIGHT: An innovative use of space combines a custom-crafted pool with a slim stone patio that provides a front-row view. Metal-framed chairs with cushions provide a sunny spot to contemplate the scenery or possibly a dip in the pool. Terra-cotta pots filled with cacti contribute a rugged natural touch that enhances this stylized outdoor setting.

A Nighttime Pool Party

* At the height of summer, plan a pool party that starts an hour before sunset so that guests can enjoy the gorgeous sky while lounging on your patio.

* Scatter small tables or benches along the patio and place several tea lights on each to create spots of brightness that won't compete with the stars.

* Stock a portable bar or ice-filled cooler with frosty drinks and frozen treats.

* Serve an assortment of cold foods, or cook on the patio grill and have guests bring cold side dishes.

* Have plenty of towels on hand for swimmers, and robes or light throws in case it gets chilly.

with creative landscaping and a roomy patio nearby. It doesn't have to be plunked in the grass out in the south forty, removed from the outdoor living area. Rather, creative design can make an aboveground pool every bit as inviting and enjoyable as one that is built in. And while we usually associate a deck with an aboveground pool, there are instances where it can be partially sunken (in a sloping area for example) and almost appear to be built in.

A built-in pool requires a sizable investment, but when joined by a stunning patio it can be an asset to even the most modest home. Built-in pools are made of concrete, premolded fiberglass, or metal frames with vinyl liners. There are practical and decorative advantages to each. One-of-a-kind designs are possible when constructing a pool of concrete, whereas fiberglass models are available only in predetermined shapes and sizes. A vinyl-lined pool can be the least expensive way to go initially but liners do need to be replaced every few years.

Style by the Pool

Built-in pools require some thought about shape or design, interior color (with a fiberglass or vinyl-lined model), and the type of trim that will be used as pool edging (stone, tile, or brick). There is also a variety of accessories to be considered such as fencing, pool waterfalls or fountains, diving boards, ladders, underwater lighting, pool games, floating devices, and a box or shed to store pool supplies and equipment. Last but certainly not least, the patio and landscaping around the pool will be a major influence on the level of enjoyment the area provides and the natural beauty it conveys.

Landscaping around a poolside patio is strongly determined by where you live. Trees, shrubs, and flower beds can have a big impact on backyard beauty in northern areas; palm trees and tropical plants predominate in the warmth and humidity of southern climes; and cacti and desert rocks can be used creatively to fashion a striking landscape in the desert. In any area flower beds and perennial gardens can provide the perfect backdrop for the shimmering beauty of a pool and an inviting poolside patio.

Fencing can contribute handsome good looks to the pool and patio area, and provides a measure of safety and privacy as well. Wooden fencing, available in many different designs, can surround the yard with a locked gate to prevent intruders or small children from wandering into the pool area. There are also ornate wrought-iron fences that are the perfect touch when the home displays vintage architecture, and high-tech plastic fences, which come in many different colors and styles, are virtually maintenance-free. Unless your home is situated in a remote or very private area, fencing affords peace of mind for anyone owning a pool. Be sure to check local laws—in some communities fencing is required when there's a pool on the property.

Handy accoutrements for the poolside patio can keep refreshments close at hand and make casual meals a snap. A mini bar on wheels can be moved poolside or can take up residence on the patio to keep drinks and snacks within easy reach—and minimize trips in and out of the

house. For entertaining and patio cookouts, an outdoor "kitchen" including a built-in sink, storge area, and gas grill is the height of luxury and convenience. For something a bit more middle-of-the-road, a portable gas grill can be kept in a convenient spot on the patio for summertime meals. Just be sure it's situated where guests won't be subjected to smoke and fumes.

ABOVE: Sometimes safety and security are concerns but privacy is not. This secluded pool and patio area is entered through a striking iron gate that's both functional and beautiful. Eye-catching black iron fencing and gates have a classical appeal that enhances almost any landscape.

OPPOSITE: A luxurious built-in pool, hot tub, and stone patio are enclosed in a large screened-in room for year-round pleasure and use. Decorative tiles incorporated into the pool and hot-tub design add a touch of elegance. Casual furnishings crafted of aluminum wear a black finish that blends nicely with the framework of the structure overhead.

Comfort by the Water

When choosing furnishings for the poolside patio, the chaise longue immediately comes to mind. Whether you are relaxing after a refreshing swim or just sitting by the water with a good book, the chaise longue is the ultimate in comfort. You may be surprised at the numerous decorative styles and modern interpretations available today when it comes to this venerable patio favorite. Remember the metal-framed chaise with colorful webbed tape that you could pack in the car to take to the beach? It's back for those who love the retro look and is available in a wide array of spirited colors. Can you recall the wooden chaise longues or steamer chairs lined up in a row on luxurious ocean liners? Choose from among several new renditions that combine solid comfort with the beauty of durable teak wood, or consider an aluminum-framed model with comfortable cushions. Even those who hesitate to give up their favorite Adirondack chair will be pleased to know that a chaise is available with all the rustic charm of that classic style. There are also adjustable resin recliners and contemporary designs that incorporate airy colored mesh with sturdy resin frames. And for those who love wicker and just can't imagine the patio furnished any other way, manufacturers specializing in all-weather wicker and resin wicker look-alikes have come up with a smart lounger that's reminiscent of a Victorian daybed.

The poolside patio is the perfect spot for a table and chairs from which to host casual family meals. Whether it's lunchtime sandwiches or a late dinner under the stars, a wrought-iron or aluminum out-door dining set makes the patio a truly versatile outdoor living space. Glass-topped tables and chairs constructed with simple or elaborate designs are a perfect addition to an outdoor setting, and the major-ity of weather-resistant pieces are made in a variety of fashionable styles and finishes. Tables are available with or without sun umbrellas and many manufacturers offer accessory items such as side tables and serving carts for added convenience. There are also tables featuring wrought-iron bases with beautiful mosaic tops crafted from colorful stained-glass pieces. These café tables are made to accommodate either two or four people for intimate gatherings with a European flair.

By combining the strength of aluminum and the timeless beauty of teak, several manufacturers have come up with furnishings for the patio that are as comfortable as they are beautiful. Tables and chairs with aluminum frames and teak slats are a sophisticated way to add drama to the poolside patio. For those who prefer all wood, there are tables and chairs constructed entirely of teak.

Unforgettable views of an ocean or a lake don't have to be spoiled by strong winds if glazed inserts are installed. This tiled patio with a built-in "window seat" is made cozy with plump cushions and pillows, a sun umbrella, and a low table for convenient drinks. Seashells make the perfect decorative accessory in a setting such as this.

Tables are usually available in round or rectangular shapes with extensions that allow them to seat larger crowds.

Assorted chairs that can be moved easily about the patio are a must for conversing, relaxing, or simply daydreaming by the pool. Wrought-iron, aluminum, teak, resin, and all-weather wicker chairs are available in different styles and can be accompanied by side tables or a coffee table for ease. There are also fun-loving sling-style canvas chairs that are perfectly at home on the patio—they're not just for the beach. And while the rocker is generally associated with the porch, who says it can't hold a proud place on your patio? The important thing is creating comfort, so by all means bring out the rocker for carefree patio pleasure.

Cushions for chaise longues and chairs should definitely be of the weatherproof variety and filled with a quick-drying material. Striped fabrics are a favorite on the patio and there are cushions available that feature stripes on one side and a solid color on the reverse. And even though furnishings and cushions made for outdoor use do stand up to the elements, it's wise to invest in vinyl covers to protect furniture when the patio is not in use.

Poolside Pizzazz

A variety of wonderful accessories for the poolside patio will enhance its appeal as an outdoor living area. For starters, nighttime lighting can be achieved with beautiful tiki torches (with a stake that's pushed into the ground) that use lantern oil or with freestanding outdoor lanterns, which are available in different heights and use lantern oil or citronella to repel insects. Votives in attractive dishes and hurricane lanterns can be used for candlelight on the table, and even wall sconces for the exterior of the house can come in handy if the patio is nearby.

When it comes to creating shade, some patios are designed with a partial overhang while others are not. For those in full sun, a freestanding umbrella with a metal base can easily be moved about where needed. Available in a variety of colors (green and white are the most popular), an umbrella can also be a decorative patio accent. Umbrellas are round or rectangular and come in different sizes to accommodate just a few or several patio guests. Netting is also available for table umbrellas to help keep pesky insects from intruding upon casual outdoor meals. Specialty shops and garden catalogs are excellent sources for these and other items that make the poolside patio more pleasurable.

The dramatic lighting in this pool and patio area is courtesy of the sunset, but once night falls, the track system in the overhang bathes the area in soft light. Outdoor lighting combined with candlelight makes any outdoor living area more versatile and enjoyable.

Swimming Accessories

For the ultimate in pool pleasure consider
the following:

✳ Foam floats and/or pool recliners
for lazy afternoons

✳ Oversize towels and plush cotton robes

✳ Portable towel stand to keep towels
handy for swimmers

✳ Sturdy basketball or volleyball nets made just
for the pool

✳ Waterproof cordless phone

✳ Water slide

✳ Workout sets for the pool (dumbbells and footgear
made with foam for buoyancy)

Landscaping is a definite plus when it comes to the pool and patio area, but what about bringing plants and flowers within close range? Unlike the deck, where you want to be able to move containers to change a focal point, the patio is ideal for large, stationary containers. Impressive terra-cotta pots can be situated around the perimeter of the patio, at the corners, along one side, or in designated areas that call for a decorative touch. Made in a wide range of sizes and shapes, such pots or containers can easily accommodate a lovely dwarf tree, shrubs, or an elegant topiary. Just be certain of where you'd like your plants to be located, since their weight will make them impossible to move. Fill in empty spaces with smaller pots of annuals and set them on the patio or elevate them from the ground in classic-looking wrought-iron pot stands with stylish curved feet.

Other ways of adding a gardener's touch to the patio include using a wrought-iron wall planter on the exterior of the house or attaching a metal planter screen to the patio and then dressing it with small clay pots held in place with metal rings. Reminiscent of the decorative screens used indoors during the Victorian era, these airy and sophisticated interpretations are a good way to add notable design to an outdoor living area.

Small details can have big impact when it comes to decorating the great outdoors. Something as simple as a coconut mat placed at the patio door to catch dirt before it's tracked indoors can be pretty as well as practical. Mats can be plain and simple, allowing the texture to speak for itself, or stenciled with an attractive design or pattern. And small details can add up to big convenience when you add a garden clock and thermometer that can easily be hung on the exterior of the home or pool house. Some models are made of terra-cotta and feature a waterproof cover, while others are molded of resin that you'd swear was old stone. These, too, are every bit as functional as they are lovely.

For snacks or casual meals on the patio, the last thing you want to be using is anything easily breakable or made of glass, especially with barefoot swimmers and sunbathers around. But you don't

necessarily have to settle for paper plates; instead, invest in some stylish outdoor dishware that's both break-resistant and decorative. Department stores, garden shops, and catalogs all cater to outdoor living and sell colorful tableware that looks like stoneware (but won't chip or break) and high-tech plastics that almost appear to be fine glassware. Add decorative place mats or a floral linen tablecloth to the outdoor dining table and you're good to go. Relax and enjoy.

A cement patio trimmed with flagstone takes on a sophisticated air. Deep blue tiles, used at the edge of the pool, reflect the colors of water and sky. To fully enjoy this attractive recreation area, crisp white patio furniture shaded with a sun umbrella encourages relaxation. Timeless, classic appeal can be seen in the decorative planter that serves as home for a well-tended topiary.

Without a doubt,

space limitations can

lead to the most creative

and cozy outdoor living spaces.

For city dwellers, whose only patch of

the great outdoors is in the form of a small

balcony or a rooftop terrace, there is immense

pleasure to be found in designing and actually

making full use of an

elevated garden room.

Granted, there are cer-

tain challenges to be

met, such as dealing

with strong wind and sun and filtering out

the surrounding buildings or skyscrapers, but

This lovely covered balcony has timeless appeal. Massive columns and urns contribute architectural interest to
the outdoor dining area, which is surrounded by tropical foliage. A terra-cotta tile floor, elegant bamboo furnishings
with an Oriental flair, and Roman shades with a traditional border
design add to the classical ambience.

by combining flowers and foliage for color with comfortable furnishings and select decorative accessories, the balcony or rooftop terrace can become a welcome retreat. It's important to remember that small spaces truly can have big impact.

Breezy Balconies

Regardless of whether home is in a high-rise apartment building, a big city row house, a penthouse, or a second-floor apartment, chances are you have a balcony. French doors or sliding glass doors often lead to a balcony that extends into the open air and is surrounded by an iron railing, low cement-block walls, or a decorative aluminum fencing or surround. Although balconies can differ in size, most are rectangular and offer floor space that will comfortably accommodate one or two chairs and perhaps a small café table for dining. Because space is limited, decorative touches should be kept off the floor to allow

OPPOSITE: An arched passageway leads to an elevated stone balcony that overlooks the coastline. A small table and casual chairs provide a place to enjoy alfresco meals with a glorious view. Simplicity is key when furnishing an outdoor space that has the benefit of such natural beauty.

ABOVE: A sturdy wooden railing encloses this cozy balcony with a pantiled roof. With plenty of space for a glass-topped table and summery steel chairs, this space acts as an intimate dining room where nature can be enjoyed to its fullest. Visitors—of the winged variety—are encouraged to stop by the bird feeder that hangs from the roof.

maximum room for your chaise longue, wicker chair, or other seating.

The architectural style of your home or apartment building is certainly worth considering when furnishing or "touching up" the balcony. Many Victorian-era buildings incorporated balconies into their designs, and ornate metalwork was favored for railings, especially in the southern United States. Between the late 1800s and the early years of the twentieth century, cast-iron or factory-produced metalwork was turned out in an abundance of styles to adorn the façades of both private and commercial buildings. From 1920 through the 1950s, modernism prevailed, and tubular iron with wire-mesh panels was common on balconies, where it replaced what many viewed as the decorative excess of the Gilded Age. Since the 1960s, balconies have often been outfitted with aluminum and wooden railings, as well as low walls made from cement blocks with open centers that provide air flow, reduce weight, and create a greater sense of space. For anyone restoring an older building, the balcony railing is often a focal point. Old iron railings should be scraped with a wire brush to remove rust, structurally repaired if need be with replacement parts (architectural salvage emporiums are a good source), and given a fresh coat of the appropriate type of paint. Wooden balcony railings can also benefit from a protective coat of stain or paint and should be carefully inspected for stability and any damage to the wood.

This cozy corner of a rooftop terrace illustrates texture at its very best. A paint-chipped French garden chair resides alongside a wooden lattice panel and a rustic side table that holds weathered terra-cotta pots. A plump pillow makes this the perfect spot to enjoy a good book or a catnap.

Furnishings for the balcony are purely a matter of choice—and space. Select pieces with a light and airy open construction rather than heavy, solid-wood furnishings that can overpower or seem out of place in small quarters. For a balcony with a highly decorative iron railing, there are lightweight cast-aluminum chairs, settees, and small tables with the period look of wrought iron. Keep in mind that a feeling of lightness is very desirable for balconies.

For something more modern and casual, a pair of canvas sling chairs can be placed on the balcony to provide a relaxing spot to read the morning paper or watch the sunset. The crisp, clean lines of fun furniture like the sling chair juxtapose quite nicely with the more industrial-looking balconies that sport cement walls or grid-pattern railings.

What about an intimate spot for outdoor dining? Whether it's morning coffee or a candlelight supper for two, a small bistro table with two slat-back Parisian chairs can be ideal. A compact table and chairs that can be folded up when not in use are perfect for the balcony. Other possibilities include a small, round occasional table spruced up with a fresh coat of paint or covered with a colorful cloth. Even a bench can come in handy for easy meals or summertime drinks on the balcony.

Big Color in Small Spaces

Once you've decided how best to furnish this outdoor space, you'll want to decorate to make it both inviting and beautiful. Flowers and foliage can turn a balcony into a miniature garden room but they must be added in creative ways so that they won't put demands on floor space. Hanging plants

Equipped with an attractive iron railing and a terra-cotta floor, this balcony is large enough to accommodate a table and six graceful chairs. The table is set for an elegant outdoor dinner, and although china and stemware have been selected for the place settings, the red and white tablecloth adds a casual air. The balcony is decorated with hanging planters and urns filled with ivy geranium in a variety of hues.

are just one possibility when it comes to adding a profusion of color and greenery to the balcony. If the balcony has a roof, suspend hanging plants from the overhead structure. If not, hardware that attaches to the exterior of the building can be used to support hanging plants, or a clamp-hanger can be fastened to a railing.

Window boxes are yet another idea for showcasing blooms on the balcony. Although some balconies are designed with just one door that allows access, others are built along a wall that includes windows. By all means take advantage of them by adding attractive metal or wooden window boxes filled with colorful annuals and trailing vines. For best results, select flowers according to whether your balcony is predominantly sunny or shady.

Special planters that attach to railings can be the perfect way to surround a cozy outdoor living space with flowers and foliage. Pine planter boxes that can be fastened to a wooden railing are available in different sizes to hold up to three or four small clay or plastic pots. They have adjustable "fits" and can be used on railings between two and five inches (5 and 13cm) wide. And for those who have an iron railing, vinyl-coated frames crafted of wire are made to hold two or three small flowerpots. They feature hooks that can be slipped right over the balcony railing. You can use as many or as few as you want.

There are, of course, other decorative options when it comes to adding plants and flowers on the balcony. For example, attractive wrought-iron pot supports can be hung on the building exterior, perhaps next to the door or below a window to create a sort of wall garden. Then, too, special planters are available that can sit on a tabletop, perhaps surrounding a sun umbrella. Keep in mind that simplicity can be lovely, so sometimes placing a weathered clay pot filled with geraniums or petunias on a small table or bench is the perfect touch.

Color can have big impact in a smaller space and there are myriad ways that color can bring a balcony to life. For starters, a sunny balcony can benefit from a small sun umbrella that provides shade as well as a heightened decorative effect. Either a freestanding or table model can be used, as long as the balcony is large enough. Fortunately sun umbrellas come in various sizes and shapes, but in extremely tight quarters a fabric awning will make more sense. These, too, are made in a wide array of colors and can be as practical as they are decorative. Custom-made awnings can be ordered to meet any size requirements and can be enhanced with scalloped or tailored valances or fringe.

This open-air balcony has been transformed into a kaleidoscope of color by the yellow bistro table and chairs and myriad flowers. A whimsical red and white chair fits quite nicely into the corner, where it's surrounded by assorted pots and decorative items. This is a picture-perfect example of how to make the most of a small space.

Something as simple as the fabric used on a plump chair cushion or toss pillow can also lend the balcony a homey feel. Colorful chintz in floral patterns is ideal for toss pillows and can even contribute romantic appeal to a cozy balcony retreat. Use in combination with a solid-color chair cushion and drape a linen scarf over a side table as an added decorative touch. Or, if bold stripes or country plaids are more to your liking, outfit seating with all-weather cushions that have a bright, summery mood.

The balcony definitely shouldn't be cluttered, for both safety reasons and heightened aesthetic appeal. There are, however, select items that can be introduced without overcrowding. Consider wind chimes to celebrate summer breezes, tabletop votives for stargazing at night, and perhaps a small woven rug for comfort underfoot.

Terraces with a View

The rooftop terrace, whether an expanse adjoining a city penthouse or a smaller area atop a converted industrial building or garage, offers an abundance of opportunities for creating the ideal living space outside. Usually clustered in the midst of an urban sprawl, buildings with the potential for sky-high terraces are an especially popular means of combining an outdoor living room–dining room with rooftop gardening or landscaping.

While the design potential of a rooftop space is the primary concern here, important practical aspects must also be considered. For example, when planning the space you should take into account how much weight the roof can support and whether or not there's adequate drainage. This is vitally important for a rooftop garden that incorporates actual garden beds in addition to containers or pots full of flowers and shrubs. Consult an architect or contractor to help determine where load-bearing points are located, and then plan gardens accordingly.

Generally a rooftop terrace involves a great deal more space than a balcony. Working up sketches of possible plans can help you determine exactly how you intend to use the terrace, what types of gardens you'd like to incorporate, and whether you should take measures to create a shaded area. A rooftop terrace can be plain and simple or quite elaborate, including everything from a fountain and formal hedges to an artificial lawn and garden statues. Your own individual concept of the ideal outdoor living space will help you determine the best possible use for the rooftop.

If you are starting from scratch, the first thing you may want to consider is flooring for the rooftop terrace. Small pebbles, outdoor carpeting, slate, and tile are all strong possibilities and each can lend interesting texture and color to this space. Pebbles are wonderful for creating an outdoor garden room, while outdoor carpeting has a modern feeling. Tile can be used to design a more traditional

Flowers, herbs, and small trees transform an urban rooftop terrace into a peaceful garden retreat. French bistro chairs can be pulled up to the small table for meals, and the lattice panel assures privacy. The cityscape offers a peek at other rooftop gardens.

A Romantic Evening on the Roof

✳ Plan a romantic candlelight dinner for two on the balcony or terrace.

✳ Situate the table for the best possible view, whether it's the cityscape or rooftop garden.

✳ Set the table with an heirloom lace tablecloth and those lovely plates you found at an antique shop for an intimate and personal setting.

✳ Fill a silver or glass bowl with water and float tea lights and fragrant flowers in it to create an unforgettable centerpiece.

✳ Cluster votives or footed hurricane lamps near the table to increase the ambience.

✳ Plan a menu that will be easy to transport from the kitchen to the outdoor dining area—perhaps a salad followed by a pasta dish or an elegant seafood casserole and a decadent chocolate mousse.

✳ Bring a portable stereo to the balcony or rooftop so that you can have soft music in the background.

✳ Allow a little extra time for stargazing.

or European setting. And the classic good looks of slate can be adapted to either a contemporary or a classical design.

Shade is a necessity on the terrace and there are options beyond the free-standing or tabletop umbrella that are worth considering. A fabric awning can be used over a portion of the terrace, or lattice panels can be used to construct a sunscreen. Lattice used overhead will filter the sun's rays, and potted vines can be trained to grow up and over the panels for even greater shade during the hot summer months. On a large terrace, an arbor might be added to create a shady spot, and on heavy-duty penthouse terraces, small trees can be planted in specific locations to provide natural shade.

Privacy may or may not be an issue when it comes to the terrace, but in those situations where some sort of privacy screen is desired, fencing, trellises, and even shrubs prove ideal solutions. These will also help shield the terrace from strong winds, and they add a decorative backdrop for furnishings and plants. Trellises and wooden screens can be used to mask the rooftop chimney and

A tropical hideaway becomes a favorite outdoor retreat when the balcony is furnished with a hammock for daydreaming. Offering a million-dollar view, this slice of paradise comes complete with a cane-back wooden chair, a pot of coffee, and a grass roof for shade. Who could ask for anything more?

vents, or shrubs in large containers can be grouped together to hide plumbing and heating hardware and equipment.

Furnishing the rooftop terrace usually calls for a variety of seating pieces and a table for relaxed outdoor meals. Some terraces serve as an extension of the living quarters, with access via a sliding door or French doors. As an outdoor living room, the terrace should be every bit as comfortable as the indoors. Even when a climb up a flight of stairs leads the way to this outdoor retreat, it can be planned with total comfort and convenience in mind. A hammock or chaise longue is perfect for relaxation, but a group of inviting chairs will be needed for entertaining guests. A table for casual or candlelight meals will make the terrace an all-purpose outdoor room. And since furnishings have to make the journey up to the terrace, lightweight (and weather-resistant) aluminum is an excellent choice. Available in styles ranging from traditional to modern to designs with European flair, aluminum outdoor furniture comes in assorted colored finishes. Add bold or subtle all-weather cushions for further comfort and decorative panache.

Rooftop Gardens

To make the rooftop terrace truly enjoyable, a garden can be planned to serve as a focal point and to soften the hard edges of the building itself and the skyscrapers seen in the distance. Not all terraces will be ideal for permanent garden beds designed with brick or connecting block edgings to showcase trees and shrubs. Because of the weight and drainage requirements involved in constructing a permanent garden, containers can be more practical and yet every bit as decorative. Weight, however, should still be a consideration when selecting pots and containers.

Large terra-cotta pots for planting small trees or shrubs can easily weigh up to a hundred pounds (45kg), but some containers made of lightweight polyurethane foam have the look of aged pottery and make a practical and beautiful alternative to their heavier counterparts. And what about smaller clay pots? They should pose no problem on the terrace and are ideal for annuals and colorful foliage. There are also beautiful ceramic containers that come in a variety of styles and designs to suit just about any decorating scheme. Thumb through the mail-order garden catalogs and visit the local nursery to get a clear idea of what's available.

Wooden containers and tubs are often preferred on the rooftop terrace because moisture doesn't evaporate in a wooden planter the way it's prone to do with clay pots (which means more frequent watering). Rectangular wooden planters are great for planting annuals or shrubs, while the larger round, square, or octagonal tubs are well suited to small trees such as flowering dogwood, crabapple, or

Tall Plants for Tall Places

Shrubs and vines that are ideal for the balcony or terrace include:

* ✳ Boston ivy
* ✳ Bush honeysuckle
* ✳ Cypress
* ✳ Flowering quince
* ✳ Forsythia
* ✳ Mock orange
* ✳ Privet
* ✳ Pussy willow
* ✳ Rose-of-Sharon
* ✳ Wisteria

Japanese maple. There are also custom-made units that incorporate square planters with benches for seating. These are especially nice in a garden "room" atop the terrace. Allow them to weather to a soft silvery gray for an aged or rustic look. No matter what type of containers you select, the important thing is to make sure that they are elevated for drainage. Assorted trolleys with wheels for potted plants, wrought-iron plant stands, and molded corners can all be used with clay pots.

Along with arranging containers for a pleasing garden view, there are other garden accessories that can contribute notable style and beauty. Add a trellis to the building wall and allow vines to have free rein, use topiary forms in containers for classic garden appeal, and make space on the terrace for a gardener's

This tiled rooftop terrace has been outfitted for comfort and natural beauty. Lattice panels add flair as well as privacy, and shrubs and flowers are joined by statuary and a decorative column for a personal touch. Two sling-back canvas chairs allow the owners to bask in the sunlight and their nature-inspired surroundings.

workbench where everything can be close at hand. Stacked with gardening tools, pots, and other accoutrements, the workbench even becomes a decorative element.

Another design element that will make the terrace a truly livable space is soft lighting. Access to electrical outlets is certainly a plus, but mood lighting can also be achieved by adding freestanding votives or kerosene lanterns that can be moved about as needed, wall sconces, and tabletop candles. Where electricity is available, mini lights strung across the terrace wall or railing can add ambience, as can a string of lights with shades of rice paper or other attractive material.

Add further decorative touches as you see fit. A wooden or metal screen can be used to partition a large terrace. A big wooden chest will come in handy for storing chair cushions and can also be used as a mini bar or for buffets. Scatter baskets full of flowering plants about the terrace and keep creature comforts such as cold drinks and a small collection of good books close by.

ABOVE: A striking architectural artifact adds a personal touch to a beautiful terrace and serves as a small table. Votives and an artistic hand-forged lantern contribute soft light and romantic ambience in equal measure.

OPPOSITE: Graceful white canopies and curtains reflect the light from the decorative tin lanterns back onto this rooftop terrace and provide some protection from inclement weather. A marble table and steel latticework chairs add a note of elegance, while container gardens contribute to the outdoorsy feeling. The owners' personal style and attention to detail have created an outdoor space that's as striking and inviting as any indoor room.

The concept of

an outdoor garden

as a living space actually

has roots as far back as the

ancient Greek and Roman civilizations.

But while these gardens and their elaborate

pavilions often had religious significance, today's

garden retreat is viewed as a pleasurable

extension of the home—a room with the ultimate

view. In light of increased

building costs and the ten-

dency to build smaller homes

with multifunctional rooms,

it makes perfect sense that the outdoors has

become a space for family time, recreational

activities, entertaining, and peaceful solitary

Evening hours can be enjoyed in any garden retreat with the addition of outdoor lighting. Decorative garden lamps, which help illumi-
nate the walkway, are combined with candlelight lanterns that cast a soft glow under the elegant canopied tent.

relaxation. The yard-turned–garden retreat answers the need for a tranquil and lovely place where we can unwind and rejuvenate our work-weary selves—all the while enjoying the natural beauty that surrounds us.

Today's garden retreats are planned in all shapes and sizes and can incorporate outdoor structures such as gazebos, pergolas, arbors, or decorative arches. They also can include fencing for privacy, paths or walkways, a gardener's work space, or paved areas. Even a small lot or a favorite corner

ABOVE, LEFT: Natural materials including stone, tile, and wood have been used to design a rustic outdoor shelter with a picture window that offers a serene view. Wooden chairs flank a table with an easy-care tile top that can be used for everything from serving refreshments to enjoying a spirited game of checkers.

ABOVE, RIGHT: A private sanctuary in a wooded landscape, this gazebo has been intricately crafted with a unique wooden floor and wood-lined ceiling. Lattice panels and gingerbread trim give it a decidedly Victorian look, and the wicker furnishings are in keeping with the period theme. Fitting decorative touches include a floral hooked rug, a hanging planter, and pots filled with flowers and greenery.

OPPOSITE: A garden bower constructed of pressure-treated lumber comfortably accommodates an elegant table for dining. Wildflowers frame this outdoor retreat, and climbing vines act as a privacy screen. The table is dressed with a lovely white damask tablecloth, and flowers from the bountiful garden are the obvious choice for a centerpiece.

of the yard can be transformed into an outdoor haven. Keep in mind that it's not the size of the land you have to work with—it's what you do with it that makes it a stylish and enjoyable living space. And central to any garden retreat is, of course, the garden.

Designing a Personal Paradise

Ideally the garden retreat combines trees, flowers, and shrubs with privacy to give it a roomlike ambience. You don't have to be an expert gardener to create a garden room, but you should have some sense of what successful garden planning entails. Nor do you have to spend a king's ransom to

create a pleasing garden room. Simplicity can often be the key to the most beautiful outdoor setting. With this in mind, combine trees and shrubs with perennials that will provide color and texture year after year, which will help keep costs under control.

Also consider your home's architectural style when planning the garden. Is your house cottage-like or classical in design? This will help you determine whether your garden should be formal, casual, or even rustic. Naturally any garden should be planned with balance in mind. Consider color, texture, and height when selecting the plants you will use.

Finally, knowing how the garden will be utilized will help you to create the perfect retreat. Will the garden be used for entertaining? If so,

---

OPPOSITE: Weather-resistant fabrics can be used to fashion a striking garden canopy with roomlike proportions. Scalloped red trim and eggshell curtains pulled back to allow glimpses of the garden give this outdoor retreat an almost formal air. Weathered wood is used for the floor, and heirloom wooden furnishings piled high with pillows encourage relaxation.

ABOVE: A beautiful rock garden and climbing roses afford a pleasing view from the simple bistro chair and table set. Whether it's drinks or dinner under the shade of a tree, this garden retreat is far removed from the hustle and bustle of the day—and therein lies its charm.

close proximity to the house is ideal. Are you looking for a secluded spot to place a bench among the flower beds? In that case, immediate access to the house is not a primary concern and the garden room can be located down a winding path.

What type of garden should you plant? Do you want it to provide you with an abundance of fresh-cut flowers for indoor use or perhaps herbs for cooking? Then plan accordingly. Granted, gardens are usually thought of in terms of flowers, vegetables, or herbs, but since there are no hard and fast rules you can combine any or all of the above to suit your needs and desires. Bulbs are an easy way of creating color in the spring and any garden retreat will be off to a wonderful start thanks to the tulips, daffodils, and crocuses you planted in the fall. Once the warmer weather arrives, you may decide to plant colorful annuals, but don't overdo it—too many flowers and a jumble of colors can feel busy instead of soothing. Favorite perennials like peonies, crested irises, hostas, or daylilies contribute color, height, and interesting texture to a garden where they mingle quite nicely with trees and shrubs. Herbs such as thyme or rosemary make an attractive addition to a cottage-style garden. Other garden themes focus on roses or rocks—the possibilities are almost endless, and with thoughtful planning and a bit of imagination you can design a wonderful garden retreat.

Regarding herbs and certain vegetables, these can often be grown in artistic or eye-catching containers placed among the flower beds. Experiment with easy-to-grow basil, parsley, thyme, rosemary, oregano, mint, and tarragon. Since herbs like the sun, select the southern corner of your garden retreat to place pots or a raised bed to grow herbs. Given generous space to breathe and proper soil conditions, herbs surprise many gardeners with how easy they are to grow and how beautiful they actually are. Visit nurseries that handle herbs for the best advice on when to plant, growing from seed versus transplants, and other helpful hints. Use attractive clay, ceramic, or wooden containers to show herbs at their best, and move them indoors when the weather turns cold.

Lush Landscaping

Gardening is one thing, landscaping another. Trees and shrubs, a patch of green lawn, a hedgerow—all can be incorporated into a garden retreat to make it more comfortable, inviting, visually pleasing, and private. Use a critical eye to plan your landscape design and take into consideration the sunlight the area receives, the direction breezes blow, and the view you want to create. Your trees and shrubs should serve as a backdrop to an open center—they create the roomlike proportions of a garden retreat.

There are three different types of trees to consider planting. While all are beautiful, small ornamental trees that blossom in the spring offer additional color and are perfect for limited spaces.

A large shade tree such as a mighty oak or a willow will provide an abundance of shade in a sunny garden, but evergreens are admired for their year-round color and beauty.

When it comes to shrubs, a natural privacy screen can be achieved in the garden retreat by planting lilac, quince, and forsythia. Not only do they help create seclusion, but they provide beautiful, colorful blooms with heavenly scents.

Once your landscape design and garden have been thought out, numerous decorative accents can enhance the space by providing easy access, privacy, shelter, and focal points. The garden that's located away from the house can be connected by an attractive path or walkway made of brick or flagstone. Even a rambling wooden walkway can become a decorative accent, leading the way to a private outdoor retreat.

Defining the Garden Area

To separate the garden room from the rest of the yard, you may decide to use a gate at the end of a path to help define the garden area. A lovely gate can stand alone as a focal point or be connected to a privacy fence. Select a gate and/or fence that enhances your garden. An ornate iron gate will blend nicely in a traditional setting while a rustic wooden fence, allowed to weather to a silvery gray,

Cottage charm reigns supreme in this appealing garden retreat. Stepping-stones lead from the back porch to the lovely curved stone bench, where a simple picket fence frames a casual floral bed.

A whimsical bower, ideal for picnicking, becomes a focal point in this cottage-inspired flower garden. A white picket gate stands open to allow visitors to wander through this lush retreat. Note how the garden has been designed so that taller flowers and rosebushes grow along the fence while smaller blooms frame the garden path.

will complement a woodland setting. A white picket fence or gate conjures up images of a cottage garden with wildflowers in full bloom. Use your imagination—a fence can be made from something as simple as willow branches bound together with wire and then used in special areas to create a rustic backdrop or privacy screen.

A stone wall is another option for creating privacy. Enclose a portion of the area with flat rocks or stones fashioned into a low wall to evoke the spirit of a traditional or cottage garden retreat. Once in place, a stone wall looks as if it's been there for years, and it can be used to train ivy or flowering vines such as honeysuckle or wisteria. While similar in many ways to a stone wall, a brick wall has a more elegant, classical appeal and would be a wonderful addition to a formal garden.

ABOVE, LEFT: A curved walkway is designed with casual floral beds and shade trees. Southwestern architectural flair, seen in the garden wall, makes a fitting backdrop for cacti and rustic willow chairs.

ABOVE, RIGHT: An elegant, custom-crafted garden bower is furnished for solid comfort and relaxation. A striking brick and tile fireplace takes the chill out of a cool day, so it makes perfect sense that wicker chairs are positioned close to the hearth. The cushioned chaise longue and mosaic tray table, on the other hand, are moved to the edge of the patio for enjoying sunny days and a view of the bright bougainvillea spilling over the bower.

Garden Shelters

A shelter of some sort has long been an important part of a relaxing garden retreat, and the gazebo has been a favorite for well over a century. Known early on as pavilions, outdoor shelters became

A Perfect Garden Party

✳ Plan a garden party for a summer afternoon, when the flowers are at their peak.

✳ Create the menu around edible flowers—perhaps a salad with nasturtiums, sandwiches with cream cheese and pansies, and a cake garnished with candied roses.

✳ Serve a variety of fresh fruit juices and iced herbal teas to enhance the outdoor theme.

✳ Situate a table and chairs in the garden, under the pergola, or in the gazebo.

✳ Scatter additional chairs and benches in the prettiest corners of the garden.

✳ Pull out the good china for an elegant touch, or opt for one of the new plastics that looks like crystal to avoid any worry over breakage.

✳ Do you know someone who plays the violin, flute, or harp? Invite him or her to play at the party.

Entertaining in this beautiful garden retreat requires little more than the perfect place: a large table dressed with a lovely white cloth and comfortable wicker chairs. While nature's beauty surrounds the spot, a trio of sunflowers in terra-cotta pots interspersed with sky blue votives enhances this yard-turned–dining room.

fashionable in eighteenth-century Europe, thanks to several noted landscape architects. They also became a status symbol of sorts for the upper class, who could afford to lavish huge sums of money on their parklike estates. Usually classical in design, these early pavilions resembled miniature temples until formal landscapes fell out of favor and rustic or romantic cottage gardens became the rage.

By the middle of the nineteenth century the gardening craze had caught on in North America, and outdoor structures, known during that period as "summerhouses," were built in a variety of whimsical Victorian styles as well as Oriental, classical, and rustic designs. Exactly when the word *gazebo* came into use to describe outdoor structures or summerhouses remains somewhat of a mystery. However, the word itself, meaning "to gaze," seems fitting for a garden structure that does indeed make the most of pleasant surroundings or a wonderful view.

A romantic addition to the garden retreat, a gazebo can be built in a variety of sizes and styles. It can be custom-made or built from the kits available at large home-building centers and lumber

ABOVE: Conveniently situated close to the house, this garden retreat has been outfitted with wicker furnishings that are reminiscent of late Victorian style. Plump floral cushions add sink-down comfort, and twin stools prove ideal for resting drinks and snacks.

OPPOSITE: A potpourri of blooms fills the floral bed that leads to this cozy summerhouse. The small cottage, outfitted with all the comforts of home, looks onto a brick patio accessorized with garden ornaments such as an Oriental red lacquer table supporting twin mirrored blue glass globes and a child's chair painted a cheerful French blue.

yards. The gazebo can be square, round, octagonal, or hexagonal and can be screened in or feature open sides. Popular building materials include wood, brick, and wrought iron with a solid roof sporting cedar shakes, shingles, or even tin. Most gazebo flooring is wood but elaborate models may feature a brick, stone, or decorative tile floor. With the recent Victorian revival in interior design and efforts to restore nineteenth-century buildings, gazebos dressed with all manner of decorative gingerbread have proved popular. If, however, you long for a summerhouse somewhat simpler in design, classical and rustic structures are ideal alternatives.

Depending upon what you'll use the gazebo for, you may want to consider adding built-in benches or even a built-in table. As with any structure, check your local building ordinances for restrictions and whether you'll need a building permit. And for those who just don't want a permanent structure in the garden area, a polyester gazebo complete with scalloped edges can be assembled for special dinners or a garden party. Made of weatherproof material and tubular steel framing, these are fairly easy to assemble and are available in stripes or solid white.

Other structures that can enhance the garden retreat and serve as a focal point include pergolas, bowers, and arbors or archways. Often used to create an ornamental walkway between two gardens or a lawn and a garden, a pergola can also serve as an enclosed space in a garden retreat for relaxation

OPPOSITE: A paved walkway leads to a Victorian-style gazebo that's been beautifully decorated for a special event. Careful attention to detail has resulted in a lovely landscape design that enhances the outdoor retreat and makes it an eye-catching focal point. White wicker furnishings provide a pleasing contrast to the natural wood finish and shingled roof of the gazebo.

ABOVE: The quintessential garden structure—the gazebo—has been popular in North America since the latter part of the nineteenth century. This beautiful example, built with latticework panels and ivy-covered posts and roof, has been made in the traditional octagonal design. Accessorized with white garden furniture and a basket of flowers, it becomes an ideal spot to relax and "gaze."

or outdoor dining. Built from wooden posts with an open-beam or lattice covering, the pergola can be enhanced by training ivy or flowering vines to grow up the sides and over the top.

Similar to a large pergola but used as a "room" within a room rather than as a walkway, a bower is a structure formed on three sides rather than two. Weather-resistant metal bowers are available with ornate latticework ideal for vines or climbing roses, and some have Victorian scrollwork that recalls the spirit of the nineteenth-century garden room. The bower can be situated anywhere in the garden to transform the landscape into a beautiful, private retreat, and it is generally large enough to accommodate a dining set or comfortable outdoor furniture.

Arbors are excellent for adding definition to a garden room. They are available in wood, metal, or high-tech resin and either have an arched

design or are built with a flat lattice roof or overhead portion. Often used to frame a garden or walkway entrance, an arbor can also be tucked into the corner of an outdoor retreat and accessorized with a bench. Depending upon the style of the arbor, it can offer a formal introduction to the landscape beyond or convey cottagelike charm. Some arbors, handcrafted of grapevine or sturdy twigs, recall the more rustic gardens of days gone by and can be every bit as beautiful and striking as more elaborate designs. Arbors make the ideal focal point in a small garden and are a cost-effective alternative to other, more expensive outdoor structures.

ABOVE: A stone path is perfect for leading the way to a cottage garden retreat. A rustic arbor crafted from tree branches showcases a vintage iron bench and becomes a striking focal point. With just a little imagination, nature's riches can be used to achieve lovely results.

OPPOSITE: A garden shelter fashioned from lattice panels, colorful painted posts, and square paving stones is dressed with matchstick shades for privacy and relief from the sun. Striped blankets and plump pillows make an inviting platform ideal for lounging.

Furnishing the Outdoors

No matter what your focal point or garden room design, you'll want comfortable furnishings in which to relax and enjoy the serenity and the beautiful landscape. Choose furniture that's weather-resistant and matches the mood of your garden. A pair of cedar Adirondack chairs is perfect for kicking back and relaxing in a casual setting dotted with wildflowers and evergreens. The soft gray patina that wooden furniture acquires over time will enable the chairs to blend into the natural hues of the landscape. Add a small wooden table to provide a handy space for a cool drink, a good book, and perhaps a pair of binoculars for bird-watching.

Also available in cedar, a bench and planter system can be used in the garden retreat. Box planters can support a bench almost four feet (1.2m) in length and generous planters can be used for anything from shrubs to annuals. Depending upon the size of your garden room, use a single bench with a pair of planters or make an L-shaped seating arrangement with two benches and three planters. Other benches, in designs ranging from the ornate to the primitive, can be used along a winding path, under an arbor, or even beneath a tree. Special benches are available to encircle trees, and the hexagonal sections of which they're composed can be assembled with weather-resistant hardware. When it comes to benches, however, perhaps the most popular bench design for the garden is the simple English cottage bench. Crafted of wood (usually cedar or teak) and sporting rectangular lines, the English cottage–style bench has been used for decades. For something more decorative, how about a cast-aluminum bench reminiscent of the wrought-iron benches used in the Victorian garden? Displaying all manner of embellishments from floral motifs to scrollwork, these high-style benches combine function with decorative flair.

All-weather wicker furnishings and resin furnishings that look like wicker are perfect for a cottage garden retreat or even a more formal space with hedgerows and classic floral beds. Wicker is also at home in a Victorian-style gazebo, where comfortable rockers and armchairs encourage lingering to converse with friends and family or simply to enjoy a serene view. If space allows, a wicker table and chairs can be placed in the gazebo for alfresco dining or garden parties.

Other outdoor furnishings made of aluminum or wrought iron are available in a wide variety of styles to suit any garden retreat. Furniture lines featuring traditional, European, and modern designs include

---

Set amid the trees, a handsome table provides plenty of space for a tray of refreshments and fresh fruit as well as garden accoutrements that add fitting decorative touches—a watering can, a vintage pail that's home to a dwarf tree, and a small succulent plant. A nearby chair is covered with a patterned throw, and a metal lantern hangs from the tree for use in the evening.

everything from tables and chairs to settees and loungers. Teak furniture, long an outdoor favorite because of its durability and beauty, is just as welcome in the garden as it is on the patio.

Tea Lights and Trellises

Numerous decorative accents can be used in the garden retreat, depending upon your personal style. For example, lighting may or may not be a necessity, but in those garden rooms where nighttime illumination is desired or where you'd like to be able to view the garden at night from indoors (to really make it an extension of your home), low-voltage lights are ideal. Decorative lanterns and post lamps can light a garden path or cast a soft glow on the garden area, while an adjustable accent spotlight can be directed upward to showcase trees or perhaps an arbor. Decorative lighting fixtures can be found with subtle Oriental designs, nautical themes, traditional styling, and whimsical shapes such as animals or flowers.

Other special touches in the garden can include everything from an ornate birdbath or an elegant fountain to cast-iron urns and metal ornaments. Add garden accents that you find both soothing and visually pleasing. Tuck them into floral beds or create a focal point on a manicured landscape. You might use decorative stone, tile, or wrought-iron edgers in the floral bed to define the separation between your lawn and garden. Blooms can also spill over a Gothic swag edging or scalloped wooden borders. Consider cast stone and tile for a more formal or traditional garden retreat, wrought iron for the Victorian-inspired or English country garden, and wooden edging for a natural or rustic garden room.

Objects and ideas abound—what about providing eye-catching support for climbing plants and vines by adding an obelisk or two to the landscape? These tall, pyramid-shaped trellises are the perfect way of adding a focal point, height, and strong visual interest to the garden room. Made of wood or metal, obelisks are available in varying sizes through many mail-order gardening catalogs.

Garden Details

* Bird feeders

* Croquet set

* Decorative garden stakes to define plantings

* Garden statues of animals or mythological beings

* Garden weather vane

* Gathering basket for clipping flowers

* Mirrored glass gazing ball on a stand

* Planters on pedestals

* Sundial on a stand

* Weather-resistant garden hose

* Wheelbarrow to display potted plants

* Wind chimes

It almost seems an understatement to say that the garden has become an extension of the home. The garden retreat offers untold opportunities for creating, nurturing, enjoying, and living the good life outdoors. With just a tiny patch of land and a bit of imagination, you're well on your way to designing the most beautiful room outside the house.

ABOVE, LEFT: A tile mosaic platform includes a rustic bench for contemplating the finer (and simpler) things in life. A twig table becomes a plant stand with the addition of a container garden, while another planter filled with yellow blooms sits on the bench. Trees and shrubs add privacy and abundant natural beauty.

ABOVE, RIGHT: The beauty and simplicity of an Oriental garden design evokes peace and tranquillity. A tall wooden fence assures private moments to listen to the water trickle from the hand-carved fountain and to admire the crimson foliage of maple trees nearby. Japanese-inspired doors provide passage into this inviting garden retreat.

When it comes to

outdoor living areas,

conservatories, greenhouse

rooms, and sunrooms truly invite

nature inside. While there are very

distinct differences among them, the one thing

these rooms all have in common is that they

serve as an extended home space where sunlight

and nature can be enjoyed year-round. Each can

be a personalized garden

room of sorts that fills

the need for a place to

Conservatories and Sunrooms

dine or entertain, relax, or carry on a favorite

pastime. And by combining climate control with

construction materials that absorb and then

release heat from the sun's rays, a wide variety

This waterside sunroom is simple but beautiful with deep red walls and trim and casual furnishings covered with white throws. Colorful pillows add brightness and complement the natural textures found in the tile floor, wood table, and wicker ottoman.

of plants can serve as decorative elements without regard for the change of seasons or the temperature outside.

The Original Glass House

What began in eighteenth-century England as orangeries—outbuildings constructed partially of glass to protect exotic plants and fruit trees during the cooler months—eventually evolved into fashionable conservatories. Not that early orangeries were crude or unadorned: many examples built on British estates had striking Oriental or Grecian designs. But it wasn't until the Victorian age that orangeries or conservatories expanded into actual living spaces.

Victorian conservatories were a symbol of refinement, proof that the family was cultured and had a deep appreciation for nature in all its glory. And it wasn't long before the conservatory moved into the realm of the middle class, who also found this exquisite addition to the home the ideal spot for entertaining or for simple, quiet repose.

While the concept of an enclosed garden room has remained steadfast in England, the conservatory fell out of fashion in North America for several decades. Of course there have been exceptions, including estates that are open to the public and the public winter gardens in various large cities that draw impressive crowds. Fortunately, the past twenty years have seen renewed interest in the conservatory as an affordable and elegant way to increase the home's living space and move some of the most beautiful elements of nature front and center, where they can be enjoyed and admired on a daily basis.

Designing a Conservatory

Today's conservatory can be custom-built, or a kit can be erected by a contractor or company specializing in this particular product. Conservatories are available in various sizes and shapes; the most common are rectangular, hexagonal, or octagonal. They are constructed with either wood or aluminum framing and glass—possibly insulated or tinted glass depending upon where you live. Highly decorative models often include architectural embellishments on the framing, such as windows that sport Gothic arches or pieces of stained glass. As always, when planning an addition to your home, check with the local building inspector or town hall regarding zoning laws, setbacks, and permits. It's also wise to consult an

---

Two different black and white patterns create an interesting and sophisticated flooring treatment for this lovely conservatory. The glazed ceiling has been draped with matchstick shades to keep the room cool. Lush plants make a perfect backdrop for an elegant table set with crystal, silver, and a delicious centerpiece of fresh fruit.

architect who can pinpoint the best place to build this addition—a conservatory can greatly enhance the aesthetic appeal of a home as well as increase its value. Generally, the conservatory will feature French doors that lead to the living room or dining room and another set of doors that allow passage between the conservatory and the yard or garden.

Decorating a conservatory involves much more than the furnishings you'll place there or the plants you'll use to make a design statement. Two primary concerns in a glass-enclosed structure are harnessing the sun's warmth and providing relief from direct sunlight. Accomplishing both goals calls for certain design elements, such as using a masonry floor to collect and store heat. Ceramic tiles or a brick floor in a conservatory not only contribute classic, gardenlike appeal but will absorb heat during the day and then slowly release warmth during cooler evening hours. Both tile and brick are long-wearing and easy to maintain. Tile is available in an incredible variety of sizes, shapes, and colors, so it's easy to give the conservatory a signature touch by designing a one-of-a-kind floor with an eye-catching border or a center "rug." With brick, you can plan an attractive floor by laying pavers in a traditional herringbone or chevron pattern.

Naturally there will be times when the comfort level in a conservatory can be enhanced by providing relief from the sun. In a glass-enclosed setting, this means using tinted glass on the roof and possibly throughout the room itself. This is especially beneficial in southern or desert areas. Double-glazed windows will also help reduce the sunlight that streams into the conservatory and can be used in northern climates where extra insulation is a plus. Check with an architect, a contractor, or a manufacturer to learn exactly what types of glass are available and which will best meet your needs.

Shades used inside the conservatory can also help control sunlight and will act as a stylish decoration. Bamboo or thinner

Tools for the Indoor Gardener

* Soft brushes for cleaning leaves and hard brushes for scrubbing pots and containers

* Assorted pots and planters

* Small gardening tools, such as a trowel, clippers, and shears

* Grow lights

* Plastic spray bottles for misting water or applying bug spray

* Reference materials, such as guides to houseplants, flowers, and herbs

* Supply of different potting soils and plant food

* Watering can with a long spout

matchstick shades are especially appropriate to a garden room setting because of their natural texture and coloring. Shades can be hung where needed on glass walls, and they can even be draped across the ceiling to filter sunlight. In contrast, a more contemporary look can be achieved with the crisp, clean lines of vinyl or fabric louvered blinds. Available in varying widths and colors, louvered blinds can be matched to any decor, although white or neutral shades may complement the open, gardenlike air of a conservatory best.

Conservatory Comfort

When furnishing the conservatory, keep in mind those pieces that are best suited to a garden-inspired setting. Wicker and wrought iron, as well as aluminum pieces that look like aged wrought iron, are all perfect and can be made sink-down comfortable with a few plump cushions. Antique wicker or modern-day renditions of old-fashioned styles set a romantic tone and blend beautifully with the lush greenery of potted plants, ferns, and

A welcome addition to this beautiful home, the conservatory becomes a weather-protected garden room. Glass and aluminum framing with a white finish form the shell of the structure while a tile floor, both practical and decorative, collects and then releases the sun's heat. Dark green wicker furnishings are surrounded by a display of plants and flowers for year-round enjoyment.

flowers. Floral upholstery cushions used in combination with chintz throw pillows can accessorize a wicker sofa or settee, generous armchairs, and old-fashioned rockers. Indulge with a wicker chaise longue for reading, relaxing, or napping. And make no mistake: wrought-iron or aluminum furnishings can be every bit as appealing as wicker—just select designs reminiscent of days gone by with curlicues, floral motifs, or scrollwork.

For meals in the conservatory, a wicker table with matching chairs or a glass-topped table with wicker or metal chairs will surely make you feel like you're dining outdoors—especially with a lovely view close at hand. Tablecloths and napkins with botanical patterns can enhance the setting—bright floral prints are perfect for casual family meals, while elegant white damasks are ideal for entertaining. A matching buffet or even a wheeled cart will make serving meals in the conservatory that much easier, and a small refrigerator is good for keeping cool beverages nearby.

Lighting in a glass-enclosed garden room can be simple or ornate. A stunning chandelier can take center stage above the table, and tabletop lamps sporting art-glass shades can be positioned for task lighting near seating areas. Wall sconces can be attached to wooden framing and serve to enhance your decorative style while providing low-level illumination. Select gracious fixtures with glass shades; fabric sometimes looks too heavy in a glass room.

Personalize your conservatory with favorite accessories. Plants and flowers are an obvious choice—select those that will thrive in your lighting conditions. Does the conservatory have the benefit of a sunny, southern exposure? If not, select plant species that will thrive in a shaded or partially shaded room. Some old favorites for the conservatory include African violets, orchids, palm trees, fruit trees, and hanging ferns, but there are many others to choose from. Plants and flowers can be used to create a focal point, but careful planning should go into their selection and arrangement. Larger plants are perfect for designing a backdrop, while smaller, flowering plants can make a wonderful centerpiece or still life grouped on a lovely stone or wooden bench. Position hanging plants in such a way that they'll create symmetry.

Other accessories at home in the conservatory include a beautiful ceiling fan, small fountains, statues, decorative containers and pots, architectural embellishments such as vintage stained-glass windows hung where they'll create a rainbow of color, sisal or straw matting in the seating or dining area, and bamboo or wire plant stands. Old garden accessories are one of the most popular segments of the antiques and collectibles market today, so visiting any sizable show should not only fill you with ideas, but will probably fill the trunk of the car as well. With a garden moved indoors, everything from vintage watering cans to old tomes on raising flowers can help personalize this wonderful space.

Greenhouse Rooms

The greenhouse room combines an extended living area with space to conduct a favorite pastime. For the gardening enthusiast a solar greenhouse allows plants to grow all year round in a climate-controlled setting that puts a personal stamp on the home.

Unlike a conservatory, which can be built in any direction, a greenhouse room requires a southern exposure. These rooms are usually rectangular with a slanted or lean-to roof and are available in kit form or in modular units that can be adapted to suit your needs. Often a greenhouse room is constructed over a patio, in place of a porch, or directly off the kitchen. And since this is first and foremost a space to nurture plants, the greenhouse room has some specific design requirements.

Designing a Greenhouse Room

Controlling temperature and humidity is vitally important in a greenhouse room, so you'll want to be able to close it off from the rest of the home. The most popular way to connect this type of garden room to the rest of the house is by including a sliding glass door or French doors. This particular type of sun space incorporates an exterior wall of the home in its design, which not only cuts down on building costs but also serves to

A well-designed greenhouse room is highly functional as well as beautiful and creates extended living space with a garden theme. Here, a lean-to roof of glazed inserts allows brick walls to retain the sun's heat, thereby reducing the owner's heating costs. Favorite plants, an easy-care tile floor, a rustic work bench, and a wicker chair complete the setting.

A porch finds new life when transformed into a cozy sunroom. Beneath the bank of windows, a low wall includes a generous ledge ideal for displaying window boxes and a collection of starfish. Stylish wicker chairs include plump, printed cushions for lounging, while a unique pottery side table keeps favorite books close at hand.

retain heat if the home's façade happens to be brick. However, if the exterior of your home is wood and you are planning a greenhouse room, check with your contractor to find the best type of sealer to protect the exterior of the house from moisture damage.

Like the conservatory, the greenhouse room is constructed with a framework of wood or aluminum (aluminum being the more popular and practical) and glass panels. The glass can be single-, double-, or triple-glazed to prevent heat loss, and the structure should ideally include vents and operable windows for an exchange of air. For shading, aluminum louvers can be placed atop the glass on the slanted roof and then manually operated to control the sunlight streaming into the room. Check with manufacturers about insulated fabrics or materials specifically used for shading and heat retention, as these are another viable option.

In a greenhouse room, you'll want a floor that is impervious to dirt and water as well as easy to clean. Brick, flagstone, and even pebbles work well, since any of these can be hosed down as needed and will also serve to retain heat. For seating or dining areas you can always add a sisal rug or a section of indoor-outdoor carpet to define space and lend a decorative touch.

Any working greenhouse needs a convenient work space and access to water. This can be something as simple as a gardener's work bench and a freestanding sink or as elaborate as a lovely unit that combines a sink with cupboard space and a work counter. Cupboards can be used to hide not only extra pots and gardening tools but also a small humidifier (used in a greenhouse during cooler, drier months), special lights for growing plants, and other equipment as needed.

Furnishings for Plants and People

A greenhouse room is much more casual than a conservatory and often not quite as large, but it certainly can be every bit as beautiful. Use attractive wire or wooden plant stands and benches for potted plants. Group them for strong visual impact and select decorative containers rather than the run-of-the-mill plastic ones. Plants and flowers take center stage in a greenhouse room, so use them to create striking focal points. During the winter months, try your hand at forcing bulbs and you'll be rewarded with colorful, springlike blossoms in direct contrast to the winterscape just outside your door. Crocus, narcissus, and tulips are relatively easy to force and can be timed so that you'll have something new blooming every few weeks. Also, consider making colorful seasonal arrangements, such as red and white flowers with greenery for a festive display during the Christmas holidays. Once you give it some thought, there are numerous ways to add special touches at special times of the year—everything from swags and wreaths to centerpieces.

The greenhouse room is the ultimate gardener's playroom, but you also want to be able to sit back, relax, and enjoy the fruits of your labor. To make the greenhouse a comfortable living space, furnish it with casual outdoor or weather-resistant pieces that won't be bothered by a humid environment. Cast-aluminum and resin furnishings are ideal in this type of garden room where they'll convey the spirit of the outdoors while standing up to a climate-controlled environment. Use an aluminum table and chairs for dining (given the lush surroundings it will certainly seem alfresco) and assorted chairs, a chaise longue, and a coffee table for a relaxed seating area. Outfit chairs with colorful, weather-resistant cushions for maximum comfort. Use striped cushions to evoke the feeling of a tropical cabana or perhaps a floral motif to enhance the image of a garden bower. Resin furniture is available in a variety of styles, but consider pieces that look like they stepped out of the English country garden or pieces that appear to be wicker. Either will blend effortlessly with the decor of an indoor garden room. Make sure to have a settee or chaise longue for napping or enjoying a good book.

When it comes to other decorative accessories, add lighting fixtures in keeping with your personal style and the casual air of a greenhouse room. Tabletop lamps, sconces attached to the outside wall of the house, and a hanging light fixture should do the trick.

Take advantage of the exterior of the house to display favorite botanical prints or framed garden posters. Check with an art store to be certain any artwork hung in a humid environment is properly framed and matted. The exterior wall can also come in handy for hanging shelves to stack garden-related accoutrements such as extra pots. Use your imagination to make this private space a favorite retreat and then sit back and watch the plants grow.

Sunrooms

Bringing the outdoors inside by adding a sunroom is something akin to having the best of both worlds. As an extended living space, a sunroom has a typical interior backdrop—thanks to a solid, insulated roof and thus a ceiling—as well as a low wall (often finished on the exterior of the room with brick or stone) that forms the perimeter of this addition. The space between this low wall—sometimes referred to as a "knee wall"—and the ceiling is, of course, filled with glass. As an indoor garden room, a sunroom offers fewer concerns in regard to climate control and shading measures.

This sunroom with panoramic views has been designed with a vaulted ceiling to incorporate added windows. The rugged ceiling and low knee wall are painted white to allow the wooden garden furnishings to stand out. Small wooden barrels and terra-cotta pots filled with plants are perfect decorative accents.

To take full advantage of the sun's heat and rays, it makes good sense that a sunroom has a southern exposure. The solid roof and a generous overhang or projecting eaves help prevent this space from becoming uncomfortably warm, while the bank of glass and windows on three sides still allows enough natural light to penetrate the room that heat can be collected by a masonry floor.

ABOVE: A turreted sitting area that adjoins a bedroom becomes a relaxing sun space courtesy of multiple windows with Victorian trim. These lovely windows have been left bare to take full advantage of natural lighting and pleasing views. Wicker chairs provide a spot for a few stolen moments of quiet repose.

OPPOSITE: This contemporary sunroom with an ocean view features a solid roof and walls of windows on two sides. Rather than designing the room with a low knee wall, the owners have opted for floor-to-ceiling glass to take full advantage of the beauty outdoors. As twilight turns to darkness, the sunroom, furnished with a long table and ladder-back chairs, is illuminated by a lovely hanging lamp.

Designing a Sunroom

Numerous companies specialize in sunroom additions or kits, although you may prefer to have such a room designed and custom-crafted. Like a greenhouse room, a sunroom can incorporate an exterior wall or may be built as an add-on. Since this is an extended living space the entire family will

OPPOSITE: Reminiscent of an Adirondack mountain lodge, this rustic sun porch features windows trimmed with birch logs. Plank walls and ceiling are joined by a floor painted red, a welcome splash of color that's repeated in the throw draped across the twig rocker. Twin ceiling fans help cool this relaxing retreat, which can be used for daydreaming or for sharing casual meals.

ABOVE: The pale wood floor of this sunroom has been dressed up with a colorful geometric-patterned rug. Playful garden motifs—such as watering cans and birdhouses—strengthen the connection to the outdoors.

enjoy, access may be off the kitchen, family room, or great room. Regardless of the climate you live in, it's wise to be able to close it off from the rest of the house to save on heating and air-conditioning costs.

As mentioned earlier, a stone, tile, or brick floor will help collect and release heat, but if this is not a major concern there are myriad styles of resilient flooring that may be less expensive but just as beautiful. You can opt for flooring with a pattern that has the look of tile or brick, or select something far different. Colorful throw rugs, sisal matting, or even an attractive Oriental rug can be used as a decorative accent. For a country-style decor, think floral needlepoint rugs or striped scatter rugs. Sisal matting enhances the casual outdoor air of the sunroom, while the muted or vivid hues found in an Oriental rug lend classic, timeless appeal.

The low wall beneath the glass in the sunroom can be painted, covered with a vinyl wallpaper, or paneled with beadboard for a wainscot effect. Select a light-colored paint or a wallpaper with a floral or foliage motif to reinforce the garden theme. While you're at it, don't forget the ceiling. Paint it white for a crisp, clean look, add beadboard for period styling, or dress it up with wallpaper. We sometimes overlook the ceiling as a wonderful way to enhance a room's decor.

A Family Dinner Among Flowers

✳ Plan a family dinner in the conservatory, greenhouse room, or sunroom—there doesn't have to be an impressive guest list to make the meal special, and it will give you a chance to catch up with one another.

✳ Set the table with the good china and silverware—make it a festive occasion.

✳ Plan a menu that includes a family favorite, whether it happens to be Chinese take-out, your famous pot roast, or something from the grill.

✳ Create a centerpiece of homegrown fresh flowers in a colorful glass bottle or jar.

✳ Add candlelight for relaxing ambience.

✳ Finish off the evening with a decadent dessert—after such a wonderful meal you all may just linger in the garden room for a board game or heartfelt conversation.

Everything is shipshape in this contemporary sunroom with a round port window and a sliding glass door that leads to an open-air deck. The neutral white walls and gray tile floor allow the view outdoors to take center stage. Accessories are kept to a minimum for a crisp, clean look, but candlelight and flowers are always a welcome addition.

Sunroom Shades and Furnishings

Window shades made of vinyl or fabric that won't fade in the sunlight can help control comfort levels. Bamboo or matchstick blinds can do the same and offer interesting textures that act as a design element. For a dressy effect, fabric valances can be added and even coordinated with the fabric used for upholstery or throw pillows.

Virtually any type of furnishing can be used in a sunroom, but keep in mind that sunlight can take a toll on fabrics fairly quickly. Scout the flea markets for tables and chairs in need of a fresh coat of paint, visit an auction for vintage wicker pieces, or put that special piece of architectural salvage to work as a base for a glass-topped table.

Cedar or teak furniture accessorized with comfy cushions is perfectly at home in a sunroom and can be painted to match any decor. With the addition of a few throw pillows, the chairs can be made just as welcoming as any seat in the house. And there are always rustic wood furnishings—a hickory rocker, a bent-willow settee, or twig tables. Use your imagination to fashion a sunroom you'll look forward to spending time in.

Other accessories that will make the sunroom more inviting include an assortment of lighting fixtures for task and general illumination at night, a ceiling fan (which can also include a lighting fixture), and pleasant scenery. Toward that end, select potted plants and flowers that will serve as a focal point or a soft backdrop to furnishings. Use lovely terra-cotta pots with molded designs or ceramic containers with painted motifs, and group plants for eye-catching impact. Add other personal touches, such as a dish filled with seashells, a collection of pottery lined up on a bench, or perhaps a vintage urn. Now you've done it—you've created a space the family will enjoy for years to come. What a wonderful way to enjoy the beautiful change of seasons!

Would you rather enjoy the outdoors from the screened porch or the sunroom? How about both? After a delectable breakfast of tropical fruit is served in the sunroom, you can move outdoors to the comfortable chaise longue for some rest and relaxation.

Source Directory

Decorative Accessories and Accoutrements

Anthropolgie
800-309-2500
Stores Nationwide
Lanterns and outdoor furnishings.

Casablanca Fan Company
761 Corporate Center Drive, Pomona, CA 91768. 888-227-2178.
Ceiling fans.

Chelsea Garden Center
205 9th Avenue,
New York, NY, 10001
Plants and decorative containers.

Design Toscano
17 E. Campbell Street, Arlington Heights, IL 60005. 847-255-6760.
Replicas of historical garden sculptures such as urns, angels, gargoyles, and the like.

Hunter Fan Company
2500 Frisco Avenue, Memphis, TN 38114.
Ceiling fans.

Marty Travis
R.R. 1, Box 96, Fairbury, IL 61739.
815-692-3336.
Authentic-looking Shaker seed boxes.

Vermont Country Bird Houses
P.O. Box 220, East Arlington, VT 05252. 802-375-0226.
Handcrafted birdhouses with old-fashioned or unique designs.

Vintage Wood Works
Hwy 34 South, Quinlan, TX 75474.
903-356-2158.
Wooden screen doors, porch doors, and decorative porch trim.

Furniture

Brown Jordan
9860 Gidley Street, El Monte, CA 91731. 818-443-8971.
Aluminum, wrought-iron, resinweave, and teak furniture and sun umbrellas.

Cumberland Woodcraft Company, Inc.
P.O. Drawer 609, Carlisle, PA 17013.
800-367-1884.
Resin Adirondack-style furniture.

Ebel Inc.
3380 Philips Highway, Jacksonville, FL 32207-4312. 904-399-2777.
Casual furniture suitable for outdoor use.

Ficks Reed Company
4900 Charlemar Drive, Cincinnati, OH 45227. 513-985-0606
Wicker furnishings.

Fran's Wicker & Rattan Furniture
295 Route 10, Succasunna, NJ 07876.
800-531-1511.
Full line of wicker and rattan furniture.

Giati Designs, Inc.
614 Santa Barbara Street, Santa Barbara, CA 93101. 805-965-6535.
Teak furniture, sun umbrellas, and exterior textiles.

The Lane Company Inc., Venture Division.
Box 849, Conover, NC 28613. 800-750-5236.
"Weather Master" wicker furniture.

Lloyd Flanders
3010 10th Street, P.O. Box 550, Menominee, MI 49858. 906-863-4491.
www.lloydflanders.com
All-weather wicker furniture.

Marion Travis
P.O. Box 1041, Statesville, NC 28687.
704-528-4424.
Oak porch swings.

Old Hickory Furniture Company
403 S. Noble Street, Shelbyville, IN 46176. 800-232-2275.
Rustic furnishings made of hickory, twigs, and the like.

Outdoor Lifestyle Inc.
918 N. Highland Street, Gastonia, NC 28052. 800-294-4758.
Leisure and outdoor furniture.

Pier 1 Imports
301 Commerce Street, Suite 600, Fort Worth, TX 76102. 800-245-4595.
Furnishings and decorative accessories for outdoor living areas. Check the phone book for a location near your home.

Winston Furniture Company
160 Village Street, Birmingham, AL 35124. 205-980-4333.
Casual furniture suitable for outdoor use.

Wood Classics
20 Osprey Lane, Gardiner, NY 12525.
914-255-5651.
Teak and mahogany outdoor furniture fully assembled or in kits.

Gazebos, Trellises, Arches, Arbors, and Fences

Heritage Vinyl Products
1576 Magnolia Drive, Macon, MS 39341. 800-473-3623.
Maintenance-free fencing, decking, garden products.

Vixen Hill Gazebos
Main Street, Vixen Hill, Elveson, PA 19520. 800-423-2766.
Gazebos and screened garden houses.

Walpole Woodworkers
767 East Street, Walpole, MA 02081.
800-343-6948.
Handcrafted arches, arbors, and fences.

Mail-Order Catalogues Featuring Outdoor Furniture and Garden Accessories

Crate and Barrel
800-323-5461

Frontgate
800-626-6488

Gardener's Eden
800-822-1214

Hen-Feathers Corporation
800-282-1910

L.L. Bean
800-341-4341

Smith & Hawkin
800-981-9888

Mail-Order Catalogues Featuring Plants and Seeds

W. Atlee Burpee & Company
800-888-1447

The Cook's Garden
800-457-9703

The Daffodil Mart
800-255-2852

Edmunds' Roses
888-481-7673

Geo. W. Park Seed Co.
800-845-3369

Greer Gardens
800-548-0111

Jackson & Perkins Company
800-292-4769

Milaeger's Gardens
800-669-9956

Seeds of Change
800-95-SEEDS

Wayside Gardens
800-845-1124

White Flower Farm
800-503-9624

Sunrooms, Garden Rooms, and Conservatories

Amdega and Machin Conservatories
3515 Lakeshore Drive, St. Joseph, MI 49085. 800-922-0110.

Four Seasons Sunrooms
5005 Veterans Hwy., Holbrook, NY 11741. 800-368-7732.

Hartford Conservatories, Inc.
96A Commerce Way, Woburn MA 01801. 800-963-8700.

Screen Tight Porch Screening System
407 St. James Street, Georgetown, SC 29440. 800-768-7325.

Vegetable Factory, Inc.
P.O. Box 368, Westport, CT 06881-0368.

Photography Credits

©Laurie Black: 23 (designer and remodeler: Neil Kelly); 17, 43 (architect: Michael Dowd)

©Fran Brennan: 40 (architect: Scott Ballard, designer: Charles Riley)

©Steven Brooke: 14 (designer: Larry James); 20 (architect: Lloyd Vogt, designer: Charles Riley); 45; 62-63 (architect: Scott Merrill, designer: Kris Childs of Kristopher); 2, 69, 129 (architect: Barry Berkus); 72 left; 133

Courtesy California Redwood Association: 54 left

©Philip Clayton-Thompson: 112 (architect: James Grant)

©Tim W. Fuller: 65 (designer: Adolph de Roy Mark); 72 right, 109 left

©Michael Garland: 1, 115 (designer: Joe Ruggiero); 31 (designer: Susan Clark); 55 (designer: Kelsey Maddox Bell); 70-71 (designer: Francine Seiniger); 74 left, 102 left (designer: Marilyn Lightstone); 74 right (architect: Tony Unrue); 83 (designer: A.J. Killawiea); 98, 99 (designer: Nicholas Walker & Associates); 102

right (builder: Jeff Seamons of JTS Woodworks); 108 (Pasadena Showcase House of Design); 121 right (designer: Glenn Hampton); 130 (Ralph Lauren Designs)

© Steve Gross & Susan Daley: 116

©Anne Gummerson: 139 (architect: Shorieh Taalat)

©Kari Haavisto: 28 (designer: Kevin Kolanowski)

The Interior Archive:
©Schulenburg: 18, 27, 61, 85, 86, 89, 95, 124, 127, 136

©Michael Jensen: 50 (architects: Geoffrey Prentiss and Jay Lazerwitz)

©Chris A. Little: 56 (architect: Patrick O. Shay, designer: Michael Foster)

©Deborah Mazzoleni: 13 (architect: Shorieh Talaat)

©Maura McEvoy: 11, 22, 24-25, 67, 76, 103, 107, 110-111; 101, 104 (garden design: Allison Fonte of Pompei AD, NYC; tent and lighting design: Lillian Mauer, Brooklyn, NY); 30, 105, 117 (designers: Lisa Stamm and Dale Booher)

©Jeff McNamara: 19 (Design: Acorn, a division of Deck House);

73; 77, 137 (designers: Jim Zirkell & Patricia Stadel)

©Ira Montgomery: 114

©George Ross: 49 (architect: Glenn Gardiner, Stylist Michael Foster)

©Keith Scott Morton: 57, 88, 93, 97, 113, 140-141

©William Bennett Seitz: 42, 47

Courtesy Southern Pine Council: 54 right

©William P. Steele: 38; 52 (architect: Herbert Bienstock)

©Tim Street-Porter: 9; 16 (designer: Roy McMakin); 21; 34-35 (designer: Brian Murphy); 5, 59 (designer: Manolo Mestre); 60 (designer: Peter Shire), 64; 78 (designer: Ron Goldman); 87 (designer: Roy McMakin); 90 (designer: Mo McDermot); 109 right, 118 (designer: Tichenor/Thorpe); 121 left (designer: Charlie Hess)

©Graeme Teague: 15

©Dominique Vorillon: 7

©Paul Warchol: 33, 36, 53 right, 81, 123, 134, 135

Courtesy Western Red Cedar: 53 left

Index